ETHNIC STYLE
History and Fashion

© 2001 Assouline Publishing for the present edition
601 West 26th Street, 18th floor
New York, NY 10001
USA
Tel: 212 989-6810   Fax: 212 647-0005
www.assouline.com

ISBN: 2 84323 290 2

Translated from the French by Deke Dusinberre

Color separation: Gravor (Switzerland)
Printed by Stige (Italy)

BÉRÉNICE GEOFFROY-SCHNEITER

ETHNIC STYLE
History and Fashion

ASSOULINE

Mangbetu woman.

THE BODY:
RAW MATERIAL TO BE MOLDED

Some animals shed their skins, others change color. Among human beings, the urge to beautify, embellish, and exalt oneself has remained universally constant through time and space. From the tip of the skull to the toes of the feet, the body provides the ideal raw material for transformations in which unbridled imagination must contend with rigid symbolic significance. Every last patch of skin is the object of some ritual or other, every last lock of hair must be in place, every last torso must be draped in necklaces or heavy breastplates. Throughout the world, the art of human finery is king—a tyrannical and obsessive one. It constitutes a veritable visual language, marking the stages of the life cycle, recounting births and deaths, immortalizing marriages, announcing rank and wealth, indicating tribal membership. The vocabulary of such finery is vast, its grammar unlimited. The animal kingdom blends into the vegetable kingdom, the supernatural flirts with the human. Thanks to bodily adornment, a man can picture himself as jaguar, bird, or elephant, a woman becomes a courtesan or goddess, the body becomes a stageset or sacred vessel. Finery marks sexual differences, underlining or even extending what anatomy already asserts. It knows how to play on appearances, surfacing where least expected, stimulating fear or excitement, arousal or alarm. Uninhibited, it employs all available resources—

claws, bones, fur, feathers, teeth, hair, shells, and base or precious metals are among its many implements. Ornamentation may be temporary or permanent, light or cumbersome; it may entail display or disguise; it may be gem, accessory, or talisman, might be tattoo, scar, or mere makeup. Adorning the body, veiling the body: skin may be tattooed, scarred, or superficially painted, the skull may be shaped, the neck stretched, feet bound, lips, ears, or nose pierced. All these practices convey the human aspiration to undergo metamorphosis as a way of refining ourselves. At a time when the Western world is desperately seeking to escape a dreadful uniformity of dress, it is important to understand the wealth and symbolism of practices from other corners of the world, a veritable language employed by people who are sometimes still dubbed "primitive." Yet aren't we all "barbaric" in someone else's eyes?

As stressed by France Borel in her magisterial study on "garments incarnate" (Le Vêtement Incarné [Paris: Calmann-Lévy, 1992]), nothing is more obscene or bestial in the eyes of so-called primitive peoples than nudity, by which she meant nudity in its formless, rawest, most primal aspect. "When an infant appears," wrote Borel, "society takes it up, handles it, dresses it, forms it, and deforms it (sometimes with a certain violence). In addition to basic care—whose very variety proves the absence of objective motivation—a profound, universal, and unfathomable urge drives families, clans, and tribes to actively modify appearances." True enough, a long list of tortures have been inflicted on babies right from their first gurgles. Newborns of the Mangbetu people of Zaire (the former Belgian Congo), when barely out of the mother's womb, undergo a compression of the skull that produces a deformation strangely comparable to Egyptian pharaohs of the Amarna period. The resulting aesthetic effect is neither gratuitous nor capricious, for it is designed to integrate the human being into a specific order. The Mangbetu outwit nature by literally sculpting the heads of their offspring, turning facial features into visual signs that are recognized by the whole community—as the skull cap is extended, the eyelids are also pulled toward the temples and the profile of the cheekbones is heightened. The head, as seat of primordial virtues, has thus become an object of visual pleasure enhanced by a coiffure that completes the ornamentation.

The Amerindian world also produced numerous examples of this cult of cranial deformation. The Mayan practice of flattening skulls may perhaps have reflected an ennobling intent, although the exact reason hardly matters. Through this eminently symbolic act, the Maya were distinguishing their children from animals by influencing the natural order of things. The same is true of practices still observed among the Kwakiuitl Indians of the northwest coast and among the Chinooks, appropriately named "Flat Heads"—they use the cradle itself to produce this change, incorporating into it a plank or even stone designed to place progressive pressure on the forehead. This type of "infernal device" can be found as far afield as Southeast Asia and the island of Borneo.

Bound feet, in the Chinese tradition.

Whereas skulls may be molded in some places, elsewhere it is the feet that are bound and atrophied. It is of course the Chinese who took this practice to an extreme, making "tinier" rhyme with "sexier." If accounts are to be believed, foot-binding began in the tenth century, reaching a kind of consecration in the sixteenth and seventeenth centuries under the Yan and Ming dynasties. The tone was allegedly set by a courtesan with strikingly tiny feet ("curved like a crescent moon," according to legend). Thanks to poets, highly erotic fantasies then focused on this part of the body. A foot had to be sleek, soft, and elegant (read: "tiny"), arched like an eyebrow, as fine as a mouth, pink as lips. Behind this bouquet of adjectives, however, lay much suffering by little girls. The terrible apprenticeship occurred in childhood, between the ages of two and twelve. An elderly woman whose life had been happy and prosperous was chosen to perform the first binding. Squeezed into increasingly pointed booties, the toes would ultimately atrophy to the point of losing all mobility. The young girl could no longer get around, unless carried on a man's back.

Beauty often follows a logic diametrically opposed to functionalism—it represents total sacrifice. Whereas lower class women went no further than a certain stage

An Ibo woman wearing heavy anklets.

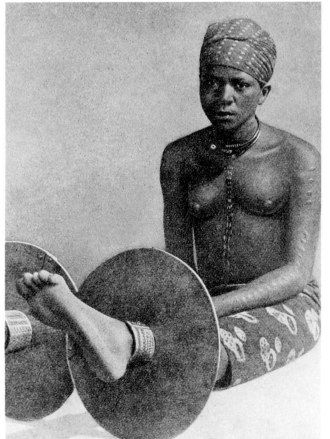

of deformation, aristocratic ladies could ultimately stand solely on the point of their heels; the ideal foot would supposedly fit in a lover's hand. Viewed as an abominable monstrosity by Western travelers in the late nineteenth century, this practice was perceived by the Chinese themselves as a form of absolute beauty. Feet had become an extremely eroticized fragment of the body (and thereby the site of all metamorphosis, and also of all violence), as well as a powerful aphrodisiac. "The more miniscule the feet, the more wonderful the folds of the vagina," went an old Chinese saying. Even better, bound feet functioned as the most efficient of shackles: women thus mutilated were forced to move with docile slowness, leaning against a wall or seeking help from a retainer or cane.

As will be seen later, the wearing of heavy jewelry—notably in Africa—could be seen as another way of restricting a woman's movement, tying her to the ground like a domestic possession or head of livestock.

Another skeletal deformation—one of the most spectacular—is the neck stretching done by the Padaung tribe in eastern Myanmar (Burma). Here again, a single feature of the female body has become a fetishistic focal point of fantasies. The extent of suffering is matched only by the scope of the sacrifice. From the age of five, a Padaung girl prepares for this metamorphosis, which transforms her not only into an object of desire but, above all, a woman worthy of marriage. Indeed, the size of her bride-price will depend on the size of the brass coil encasing her neck as tightly as a breastplate. Alas, this seductive apparel—so "barbaric" in the eyes of Western observers, who nevertheless expected their own wives to be corseted—could sometimes become a veritable instrument of chastisement and torture. Woe to an unfaithful "giraffe-woman," for her cuckolded husband would remove her neck coils. The muscles of her neck being too weak to support the weight of her head, this punishment inevitably led to death.

In other regions, it might be the lips, nostrils, and ears—those parts of the body responsible for speech, breath, and hearing—that are irreversibly enlarged by wearing heavy ornaments. Once again, the proverb seems to require that "you have to suffer if you want to be beautiful."

The use of spectacular devices (rings, plates, lip plugs) forces the body to grow, extend, dilate. Finery is inscribed in the body to the

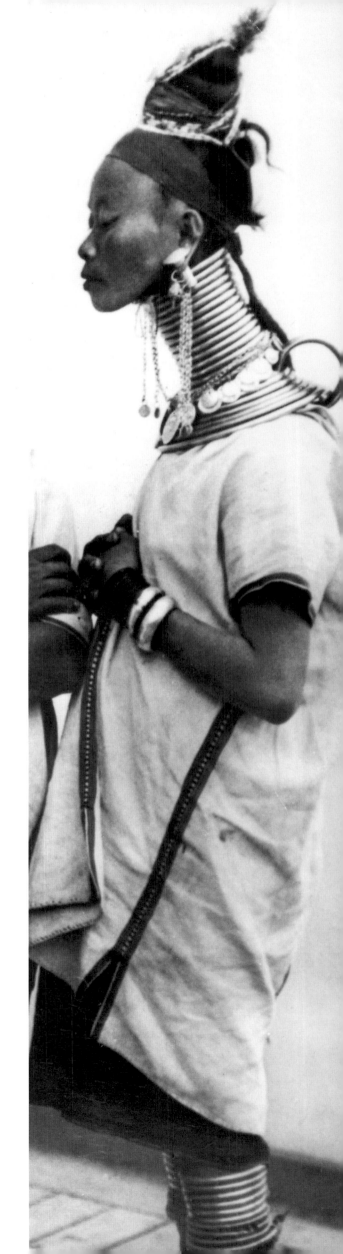

Giraffe-woman. Burma.

point merging with it: adornment and adorned become one. Here again, no materials are overlooked—beads, feathers, seashells, pieces of metal (or wood, reed, or raffia), the teeth of dogs or warthogs, the claws of carnivores, tortoise shells, stones, and minerals are all used to pierce nostril, earlobe, or lip in an apparently limitless range of visual effects and possibilities. The vocabulary of shapes seems equally limitless—disks, cylinders, rings, coils, half-moons, and so on.

on the banks of the Chari River that this practice finds its most spectacular illustration. Among the Sara, a little girl around the age of eight or ten has her lips perforated by her future husband. Her anatomy will be so considerably altered by saucer-shaped plugs that many observers find it repulsive; indeed, although it enhances their sex appeal within the tribe, wearing these gigantic plates in their lips allegedly protected Sara woman from slave raids by Islamic peoples. On this subject,

Mutilated teeth. Minwoul, circa 1905.

Sara woman at a beauty competition, 1925.

The line between seduction and repulsion is fine, as proven by countless practices ranging from accretion to mutilation. The lips are probably the part of the body most heavily subjected to this terrible game of transformation—they may be made up, tattooed, pierced, elongated, dilated, permanently deformed. The wearing of labrets, or lip plugs, may date back to Neolithic times; ancient vestiges of stone plugs have been excavated in Chad along with other objects carved from quartz. And it is precisely

Borel has correctly pointed out the close link between ritual operations on lips and female genitals: her new appearance, at the cost of true suffering, indicates a woman's change of status and sexual maturity.

Some purely religious motives can nevertheless be discerned behind the wearing of labrets. It has been claimed that these highly symbolic ornaments are closely linked to the creation myth among the Fali people of Cameroon. By piercing the lips of a prepubescent child, the community gives her the future appearance of a toad, a sacred animal who taught the first woman to speak. Here, adornment equals transmission of knowledge, becoming a vehicle of tradition. Thus when a Fali woman dies, her lip plugs are recovered a few days after death and are given to one of her daughters or sisters.

Among the Makonde of Mozambique, both men and women wear labrets as a sign of ethnic identity, meaning: "They are Makonde; they're not monkeys." The sexes differ only in material used—little pieces of wood for men, disks of metal or ivory for women.

The Americas are also familiar with "lip jewelry," according it great virtues. Carved from crystal or turquoise, lip plugs were once an attribute of the gods, the prerogative of the noble and powerful. The Suia tribe of Brazil, meanwhile, endows them with virile, warlike properties—indeed, their labrets are often red, the color associated with the fury of combat.

Ainu women from northern Japan go one step further by adorning their lips with "permanent ornaments" etched into the skin, namely tattoos. In their view, nothing could be more obscene than a woman with pink lips! Early travelers were amazed to discover this moustache-like pattern drawn around the mouths of Ainu women. Many hypotheses have been proposed to explain this singular practice. It might represent the vestiges of an ancestral world bound up with animals (women, in a troubling relationship with a frog-demon, reportedly appeared in days of yore in the form of a blue-spotted trout); or it might be a rite of passage (a woman's mouth must be tattooed prior to marriage); or it may play a curative, propitiatory role (marking the lips allegedly wards off evil spirits even as it cures rheumatism); or perhaps it merely reflected a wish to be haughty and elegant. Lip tattooing may stem from some or all of the above, pace the missionaries who virulently condemned this "barbaric" habit.

Other spectacular ways of "showing off" the mouth

Tattooed Ainu woman, circa 1900.

include mutilation and sundry dental incrustations, as practiced by various civilizations across all ages and continents. The Maya—already mentioned for their propensity to deform the skull—filed their teeth with sharp cutters and set them with precious stones, notably glittery pyrites, obsidian, turquoise, mother-of-pearl, and highly prized jadeite.

According to research conducted by Mexico City's National Institute of Anthropology and History, over sixty designs were common! In Africa, an abundant imagination once again seems to govern the embellishment of both male and female smiles. Africans do not hesitate to plane, file, or incise teeth, indeed to pull them out (the removal of the lower incisors is common practice among the labret-wearing women of Chad). Among the Tiv people of Nigeria, teenaged boys have their teeth carved by a carpenter, a tricky and painful operation that proves their valiance in the eyes of the girls!

Adornment can not only be castrating (such mutilation elevates the body the status of cult object), it also excels in what France Borel calls "aberrant" practices. One need think merely of a variety of ornaments whose size, weight, or material permanently modify appearance, even in the short term. Particularly unusual are the "cheek ornaments" proudly worn by men of the Fang people in Gabon and Cameroon: shimmering parrot and rooster feathers, shafts of raffia and bone, rings of bronze, and strings of beads attached to the hair all combine to create a most spectacular accessory.

Yet it is perhaps the continent of Oceania that best demonstrates the subtle play of appearances bordering on the fascinating and ambiguous world of animality.

Among the Asmat of New Guinea, men's nostrils are appareled in extraordinarily "savage" ornaments, namely the canines of wild boar (an animal especially valued because its skin is black, the same color as that of humans). These teeth accentuate a warrior's bestial nature even as they underscore his bravura. Sometimes a large, hollow pig bone is used for the same purpose.

Ear jewelry, meanwhile, spurs obvious sexual allusions. Many societies have made a fetish of this tiny piece of flesh, to the extent of having it indicate not only rank and confraternity, but also—and above all—of the passage from one state to another. In southern Kenya and northern Tanzania, Masai women would not be seen in public without their magnificent beaded ear ornaments, a mark of both status and wealth. Woe to her who allows herself to be seen naked! Among the Songhai of Gao, earrings seem to play the role that engagement rings do in the West. At the onset of menopause, meanwhile, Peul women in Mali must give up the garlands of jewelry draping their lobes, retaining only one item.

Men are not to be outdone when it comes to adorning the organ used for listening to the wind or the voices of spirits. In Brazil, for instance, the Suia people of Mato Grosso distend their ears with heavy ornaments, the better to hear—and therefore to understand.

In India and throughout Asia, statues of Buddha generally display long earlobes, a symbol not only of wisdom but of the Enlightened One's previous existence as a prince, when he wore magnificent jewels. Even today, the Iban people of Borneo continue to boast earlobes that reach their shoulders.

(top) Young Nuba woman. Southern Sudan, Kordofan, 1949.
(middle) Orejan Indian. North America.
(bottom) Amanab man. Melanesia, Sepik region, Iafar.

WRITING ON THE SKIN:
TATTOOS AND SCARIFICATION

"You shall not make any cutting in your flesh on account of the dead or tattoo any marks upon you," reads the Old Testament book of Leviticus (19:27). The same injunction is repeated later: "They shall not make tonsures upon their heads, nor shave off the edges of their beards, nor make any cuttings in their flesh" (21:5). There can be no doubt, then, that in Christian lands, body art is seen as an insult to God's creation, as violence done to the "natural" body.

In the eyes of colonists and missionaries, "primitive" peoples who displayed tattoos and scarring on their skin were indeed diabolical creatures whose practices had to be eradicated forever. Yet even though these Westerners viewed modification of the body as an infamous mark of "uncivilized barbarians," it was paradoxically perceived by the "savages" as the very mark of civilization.

So let us take a closer look at some clay heads modeled in Africa over ten centuries ago. Shaped by the expert hands of an anonymous potter, the full, delicate faces from the kingdom of Ife received the insult of a scar in the form of "cat's whiskers," whereas a round little face from the Sao region (between modern-day Chad, Cameroon, and Nigeria) mobilized a subtle play of lines and hatchings into an amazing alternation of ridges and valleys. As a reflection of actual practices, these touching models reveal the importance Africans have always placed on skin, a veritable medium of marks that function as so many codes. Long, sinuous scars not only underscore the intensity of facial features, they are also the mark of allegiance to clan or tribe, and a sign of power.

Transmitted from generation to generation, constantly re-etched onto new flesh, these grids, incisions, swellings, and scars thereby express the relationship between tribe and individual, record the different stages of the life cycle, immortalize both joy and suffering, and proclaim an individual's place in the cosmos and relationship to the spirits. As Michel de Certeau quite rightly pointed out, "From birth to mourning, rules 'take hold' of the body and turn it into a text. Through all kinds of initiations. . . they transform it into the tablets of the law, into a living picture of customs and rules, into an actor in a play staged by the social group. . . . In order for the law to be etched on the body, an apparatus must mediate the relationship between one and the other. Tools therefore go to work on the body from instruments of scarring, tattooing, and primitive initiation down to those of justice." ("Des outils pour écrire le corps," *Traverses*, April 1979).

The fine turn of phrase, "go to work on the body," conveys the suffering involved in such practices. The issue is ultimately skin deep, because unlike the temporary adornment of makeup and body paint, tattoos and scars permanently alter cutaneous tissue. Scarification chisels the skin with all the violence of an incision, while tattooing needles it with small pricks of colored pigment.

Another noteworthy difference is that scarring is usually practiced upon dark skin, where it plays on an alternation of ridges and hollows,

Woman with scarring on her chest.

whereas tattooing favors lighter skin against which it will stand out.

Despite these visual differences, the function nevertheless remains the same: to inscribe the flesh in a painful but permanent way with a mark of the past, of membership in a group, of social or marital status, of sexual maturity or bravery.

In many societies, the rites of inscribing begin at birth and continue even after death. Thus, Senufo babies in Sudan receive two marks on their thighs by way of protection—the cries of the newborn prove that a deceased spirit has been reincarnated. The Chibaks of Nigeria, meanwhile, make slight cuts on the forehead of their offspring to spare them an excess of blood; here, scarring plays a therapeutic role.

But it is during the onset of puberty that these "ideograms in flesh" come into full play. Given their indelible quality, African scars irrevocably mark the distinction between male and female. They also mark an individual's passage to an adult stage, inscribing each stage into the skin itself: circumcision, excision, marriage, procreation, mourning. Furthermore, they confirm membership in the social order, concretizing separation (of child from mother) and division (into age and sex groups).

Marking the skin is performed far from profane eyes and is often a highly delicate operation. Perceived as dangerous—blood does flow, after all—it often entails drugs or pain-relieving substances.

Hence, from adolescence onwards, Tiv youths in Nigeria see their bellies adorned with a multitude of concentric circles running from the neck to the navel, that vital

Young man with deep striped scars on his cheek.

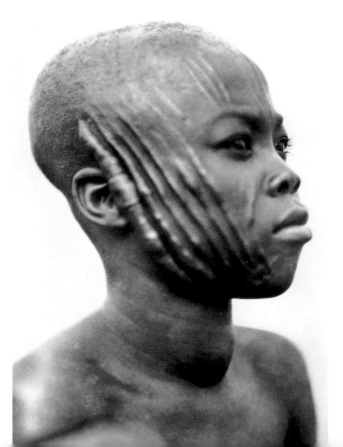

organ par excellence. It is no coincidence that this feminine mutilation is performed by circumcisers. The patterns and inscriptions are a veritable language, scrupulously indicating age group. The chests of young men are printed not only with geometric designs, but also with the outlines of scorpions and lizards.

By remodeling the body and raising the skin to the status of sculptural matter, scarring also plays a fully erogenous role. Centered on the belly and thighs of a woman, the scars draw the eye the better to focus desire. Women in Mozambique even go so far as to scar the edges of their pubis in order to enhance their sexual attractiveness. Young Tshokwe women in eastern Angola also undergo particularly painful scarring—away from male eyes—supposed to make them even more beautiful: spectacular, thick scars known as keloids stand out in high relief all around the groin region.

It is hard to overstate the aesthetic value attributed to these deeply etched designs. The variety of their visual vocabulary defies imagination; as patterns circulate, some designs are copied, while others are dropped. In one place, scarring will be done in short, fine lines which are more or less dense, more or less singular; in another, vigorous slashes scar the cheek, furrow the forehead, or chisel the face, or horizontal lines may stripe the body, accentuate the verticality of the back, or underscore the swell of buttocks. As Christiane Falgayrettes-Leveau so aptly put it in *Corps Sublimes* (Paris: Éditions Dapper, 1994): ". . . some lines deepen, others fade. Shapes emerge, sometimes intertwine or disappear only to recover their movement and attack another area of smooth skin. And all these designs strive to create the pattern of a weave, or the traces of concealed rivers and forests, or the record of human lives." Whether protective or therapeutic, magic or initiatory, erotic or purely aesthetic, these marks are printed on male and female bodies like so many pages of live text for our inspection. It is up to us to assess their symbolism and appreciate their unsettling beauty.

A Maori chief, his face covered with tattoos.

Thousands of miles from Africa, other peoples have also turned their skin into ornament. Throughout eastern Oceania, notably on the Marquesas Islands and New Zealand, men and women of the late eighteenth century flaunted extremely spectacular tattoos, sometimes covering their entire bodies. Samoans, for example, were known for the designs on their buttocks; Tahitians tattooed curved lines on their thighs, stars or circles on their chests and arms; Maoris chiseled their faces with deep, swirling incisions. These abstract and figurative decorations fascinated early European visitors—including the famous mutineers from the *Bounty*—sparking a veritable vogue among sailors and the poorer classes back on the old continent.

The very term "tattoo" allegedly derives from a Polynesian word, *tatu*, which means "drawing," and may represent a doubling of the verb root *ta*, meaning "to strike" or "make a cut." Tattooing constitutes a violent attack on the body, and is designed to leave an indelible mark—second thoughts are not an option. In order to get to the heart of the epidermis, a tattooer strikes the skin with a cutting tool (a

piece of obsidian, tortoiseshell or seashell, human or fish bone, shard of glass or metal, etc.), previously dipped in some pigment or other. In his *Voyage of Discovery*, the English explorer James Cook described the extreme violence of the procedure, which resembles a rite of initiation in many respects: A man called Tahoutai sat on the ground, the upper part of his body thrown back, leaning his head on the knees of another man who held him still. The tattooer, kneeling next to Tahoutai, used a little hammer to pierce the skin with the steely needles of a comb that he dipped into a colored substance from time to time. Thus hammered, the comb progressed temple to temple, tracing a bloody halo across Tahoutai's forehead. The painful contortions of his blood-blackened face, the nervous twitch of his limbs, and the steady lament fueled by the comb's bite revealed the suffering it cost Tahoutai to adorn himself in this strange and indelible national ornament.

As though the operation of tattooing were not already painful enough, in some regions people go even further by attacking the most sensitive parts of the body, namely tongue, penis, lips, and eyelids. Acquiring these tattoos thereby supposes both outstanding courage and submission to the elders or chiefs who insist on this ordeal. These practices, not unlike other rites of passage such as circumcision and nose-piercing, are designed to make the body stronger, tougher, and more attractive in the eyes of the opposite sex. Western travelers to the Tonga and Marquesas Islands thus realized that men with "des-

Tattooed woman from the Marquesas Islands, 1869.

perately bare" skin would not enjoy the sexual favors of their female counterparts, who openly despised them. The same dishonor apparently befell women whose lips remained pink, judged to be repulsively ugly.

Although clear relationships exist between tattoos, sex appeal, marriage, and virility, this 'permanent makeup" obviously transcends the beauty factor alone. Among many peoples of Oceania, tattooing constitutes a crucial event as important as birth and death. Being tattooed means literally modifying the appearance of the skin, wrapping the body in a new, artificial skin. Nicholas Thomas, a great specialist in Oceanic art, has rightly stressed the teeming nature of tattoos in the Marquesas, where a veritable "fear of the void" invades the skin. "The most striking feature of Marquesan tattooing is the sheer multiplication and density of designs. Marquesan men were, for the most part, warriors, and the elaboration can be read along the lines suggested [earlier] for Asmat

shields: given the movement of the body, and the structured but unstable organization of motifs, the warrior invests himself with a form of visual armor that distracts and ideally disorients his opponents. Given that a competitive warrior ethos was more accentuated in the disorderly and conflict-ridden Marquesas than the comparatively more stable societies of Tahiti, Tonga, and Mangareva, it might confidently be expected that Marquesan tattooing would be more elaborate" (*Oceanic Art*, London: Thames & Hudson, 1995, p. 104). Thomas takes his analysis one step further by stressing the eminently symbolic nature of this primal marking. Tattooing mitigates everything about the body that might be unstable and "taboo"—another word of Polynesian origin—by wrapping it in images (a series of eyes, for example, with evil-averting properties). Being tattooed meant covering the skin with an additional shell in order to limit the risk of any contagion. Many tattoos in the Marquesas therefore feature turtles, the perfect example of a shell-protected animal. "In Samoa," adds Thomas, "the final tattoo element to be applied to the body covered the navel; this can be seen to consummate the closure or armature of the body, and replaces the physical trace of natural birth."

Marquesas islanders, meanwhile, go as far as peeling the skin off corpses in order to efface all traces of tattooing prior to burial. This is probably meant to endow the deceased with the absolute, bodiless purity that is the prerogative of immortality in the world beyond.

Yet if anyone has elevated skin decoration to the status of masterpiece, it is undoubtedly the Maoris of New Zealand. The countless engravings produced by artists who accompanied Cook's expeditions suffice to reveal the amazing appeal of this "living ornamentation." Although women were tattooed only on lips and chin, men might be adorned from the waist to the knees. Facial tattooing, considered to be sacred, was apparently reserved for high-ranking individuals, and was known by the term "moko." Far from being random, the pattern of skillful, complex lines revealed a person's intrinsic identity and functioned as his "facial signature," so to speak. Whereas the same patterns might be found on all the men of a given community on the Marquesas Islands, among the Maoris designs were personalized, as demonstrated by the fact that as late as the nineteenth century these designs were still being used as signatures at the bottom of administrative documents! The particularly tricky process of facial tattooing took place in secret, far from prying eyes; the tattooed dignitary was "tab00" during the entire time the operation took place, and would be fed with the help of a carved funnel.

Styles of tattooing traveled from island to island or circulated from group to group. There is no need to be a specialist to spot resemblances between a pattern tattooed on the skin and a decoration carved on a piece of bark or the beam of a house. The same decorative exuberance can be detected on sculptures and fabrics, abolishing any hierarchy between the human body and other art forms. In the Marquesas, the form of a fish hook might appear on cheeks and neck (a sign of vengeance, according to a report by the French Dr. Tautain, governor of the island from 1891 to 1897); in Hawaii, a row of dots around the ankles serves as a charm to ward off sharks; in Tahiti, the lower buttocks are uniformly darkened in the form of two upward-pointing crescents. Among the Maoris, the parts of the body to be covered are divided into zones, themselves subdivided (some ethnologists interpret this ideal symmetry as an allusion to the primal oppositions that govern Maori philosophy: life/death, tapu/noa, etc.).

Obviously, most of these patterns have now lost their original symbolism. They can nevertheless still embody a veritable ideology that transmits other codes and promotes other claims. Samoans living in the United States, for instance, express their ethnic pride by displaying their tattoos, which represent, in a way, the essence of their identity. In New Zealand, young Maoris are returning to ancestral practices by sporting traditional designs on their faces and bodies. As in Western soci-

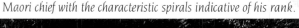

Maori chief with the characteristic spirals indicative of his rank.

ety, tattooing is shifting from one class to another, undergoing mutation, inventing new codes. No longer the prerogative of dominant castes, tattoos are now sported by the most underprivileged circles—Maori gangs in New Zealand now freely draw inspiration from the swirling lines of facial mokos, but only to express their status as outcasts! Thus, in a strange return to origins, this insolent "skin jewelry" has recovered its initial function of wrapping the body in "visual armor" (to use the phrase favored by ethnologist Nicholas Thomas).

Meanwhile, a most unusual custom has survived in Japan: on October 1st of every year, members of the firemen's confraternity parade through the streets of Tokyo. Hailed as national heroes for their skill and valor, the firemen boast amazing tattoos that run from head to foot, like a second skin. Lions, tigers, and dragons—animals known for their virility—dance across these muscular bodies, turning their hosts into veritable walking artworks.

Few countries, in fact, practice tattooing with the same passion as Japan. The first Western travelers to stumble into Japan fell under the charm of "embroidered skin," which served as a replacement for clothing. Ever in search of exoticism, nineteenth-century French author Pierre Loti willingly subjected himself to the experience, opting for "a highly unusual blue and pink chimera, which would make a pretty effect on my chest on the side opposite the heart," as described in his novel, *Madame Chrysanthème*. The operation lasted an hour and a half—"an hour and a half of irritation and pain," if the daring writer is to be believed. But what most struck foreigners in Japan in the late nineteenth century was undoubtedly the impressive number of Japanese who flaunted magnificent designs. Far from being the scandalous mark of outcasts, as tattoos were in the West, in Japan they seem to have spread "quantitatively and qualitatively" over a wide range of torsos, shoulders, and backs, appealing to various social groups from grooms to courtesans, from litter-bearers to actors.

And yet nothing is more mysterious than the alleged origins of Japanese tattooing. The geometric patterns surrounding the eyes and lips of Jomon pottery figures perhaps represent the earliest trace of this bodily adornment, dating back some ten thousand years. Caution is required, however, for such marks might also

Above: Detail of a Japanese tattoo on a man's back, "onizawa" style.
Opposite: Detail of a Japanese tattoo, circa 1900 (in Les races humaines, Editions Hachette).

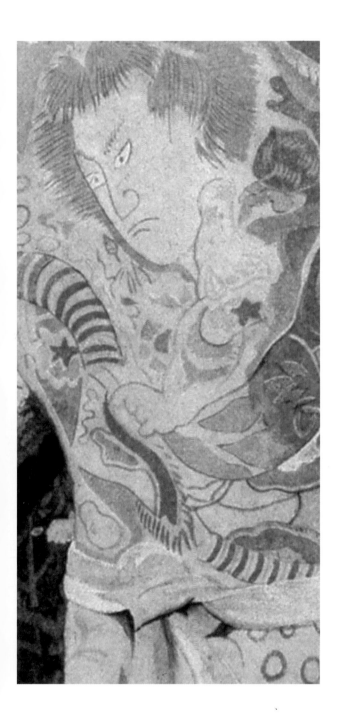

indicate ritual paint or makeup. The first written reference to the practice appears in a Chinese chronicle of the second half of the third century, which devoted a long chapter to "the barbarians from the East." Worn on the face and body, such marks allegedly played a propitiatory and magic role before becoming purely ornamental. Originally, then, tattoos were worn mainly by fishermen who "sheathed" their bodies to protect themselves from the most dangerous sea creatures.

Historians are nevertheless divided over the actual path taken by tattoos in reaching Japan. Some people cite the influence of the Ainu, a people famous for tattooing their women with a strange "moustache" around the lips. Others argue, instead, for influence from China—tattooing was a form of punishment in ancient China, along with death, castration, and the amputation of nose or feet. As late as the nineteenth century in Kyushu, Japan, the ideogram "dog" was still being tattooed on the foreheads of thieves; in Kyoto, a double bar was etched on the upper arm; in Nara, a double circle on the biceps. Even though initially a sign of opprobrium and stain, tattoos became ornamental symbols. Some writers try to explain this shift from a punitive to decorative role by the fact that criminals sought to "mask" their infamous brand by superimposing a rich pattern over it. Tattooing went from being a sign of exclusion to one of inclusion, a sign of recognition among an entire range of the population. Craftsmen, firemen, carpenters, litter-bearers, professional gamblers, actors, and prostitutes adopted tattoos in a mood of protest, ignoring all prohibitions and dictates. Tattoos for protection, tattoos for bravura, tattoos for oaths, and tattoos of love began blossoming on bodies despite the many prohibitions decreed by the shogun's government. Little did the law matter: a courtesan etched her body with the family emblems of her lovers until there was no inch of virgin flesh left; a hawker or rickshaw-puller might attract customers' attention by extravagant designs that served as advertising; a tobi (fireman) would cover himself with dragons spitting fire as terrible as the ones he had to extinguish. Having emerged among the lowborn, within the shady world of courtesans, actors, and the rabble of gangsters and gamblers, tattooing could afford to be daring, refusing to shy away from the vulgar, earthy, or erotic.

It was thus that the nineteenth century gave birth to what the

Japanese themselves dubbed "the new tribe of tattoo people." This tribe had its codes of recognition, its laws, its aesthetics. The collective movement arose nowhere other than Edo, the imperial capital. Edo the impertinent, the teeming, the voluptuous: Edo meant the plush world of geishas and courtesans; Edo reflected the artificial light of theaters and actors with their ghostly makeup; Edo harbored the famous

A ceremonial costume known as the "maghzen," Meknes.

engravers of prints that glorified the frenzy of illusory pleasures. If Philippe Pons is to be believed, "tattooing was an expression of a period of decadence simultaneously marked by the imagined fear of the end of the world and aspirations for rebirth. . . . The taste for the present that had driven Edo's culture tended to evolve into a kind of exaggerated dandyism as though flirtation and a taste for illusion were henceforth fueled by a profound feeling of the fleetingness of all things, the unrealness of a world shaped by Buddhist concepts. This aestheticism of pleasure tainted with despair, of tasteful love (as opposed to the passionate love that formerly led lovers to commit double suicide), found its equivalent in the common people's attraction to the artifice of tattoos, the expression of plebeian bravado, the dandyism of a poor wage-earner who does himself proud by decorating his only possession—his own skin" (*Peau de brocart: Le corps tatoué au Japon* [Paris: Seuil, 2000]).

It would nevertheless be a mistake, once again, to underestimate the profoundly symbolic dimension to this act of etching the body in so irrevocable a way. A look at the vast iconographic repertoire of Japanese tattoos provides convincing proof of this symbolism. One recurring figure is the dragon, an aquatic animal that breathes fire, thereby incarnating the totality of the world, the synthesis of extremes, yin and yang. Cherry blossoms, though milder in appearance, nevertheless symbolize the fleetingness of life and allude to the precarious existence of samurai warriors who might die in battle at any moment. Peonies, meanwhile, were associated with gamblers—and therefore virility—whereas chrysanthemums were invoked for their medicinal virtues. Chests and backs might also harbor a vast bestiary of phallic serpents and lascivious squid, not to mention tenacious carp and powerful Chinese lions. Signs of the zodiac and religious motifs were also highly prized, such as Kannon, the god of compassion, and Fudo, god of anger and ferocious guardian of hell. The main source of inspiration for Japanese tattoos, however, was without doubt the colorful ukiyo-e prints, "images of the floating world." The connection is perfectly logical, since the earliest tattoo artists were also engravers who used their clients' skin as virgin space suited to the full expression of their lively talent. Right from the early nineteenth century, there was fertile exchange between the arts of printmaking and tattooing. Even the great artist Utamaro was allegedly ready to try his hand: finding himself lacking inspiration one day, this famous portrayer of courtesans secretly went to a brothel to spy upon a famous tattooer working on an equally famous prostitute. Although tattoos on women were long found solely on a certain category of professional, they have always inspired the imagination of writers. "There is perhaps an erotic tone to tattooing's emphatic reminder of the body," pointedly mused Philippe Pons. The intimate and profoundly carnal bond between tattooer and tattooed woman has been the subject of countless stories and films in Japan, from novelist Jun'ichiro Tanizaki to director Yoichi Takabayashi via English filmmaker Peter Greenaway. All glorify the power of a rite in which pain is allied with orgasm. True enough, the permanent, official attire of tattooing underscores more than it masks, thereby considerably enhancing sexual attraction. Yet in addition to its power of attraction, it nevertheless remains what France Borel called "an answer to the anxiety triggered by the amorphous, formless substance of humanity . . . [it acts as] a talisman, protecting and structuring a savage, beastly life." The more poetic Pons prefers to see tattooing as "the expression—etched on the skin—of the darkness we all carry within us."

Oscillating between ornament and talisman, tattoos have always met with enthusiasm in Arab lands. It is generally thought that this type of body decoration dates back to Neolithic times in North Africa, thereby largely predating Islam's arrival in the area. Although the Islamic religion's respect for divine creation led to disapproval of tattooing, it has never been formally outlawed. Sidestepping religious objections (notably verse 118 of sura IV, which certain zealous commentators interpret as a violent denunciation of tattooing), Muslims have assumed the right to mark their skin with ornamental signs that employ an endlessly intriguing formal vocabulary. This visual idiom may perhaps be a vestige of imagery inherited from the pre-Islamic, indeed prehistoric, period. Formerly practiced on various parts of the body, tattooing is today limited to chin and forehead. Furthermore, observation reveals that it is generally lower-class women who adorn themselves thus. So does tattooing represent a tribal mark, a sign of sexual distinction, or simple finery? The original meaning of tattoos in Arab lands has yet to be firmly established. Some ethnologists now recognize its basically preventive role among people whose ancestral fear of the "evil eye" continues to worry them. North African women therefore often call upon the services of a professional tattooer to ward off problems of eyesight, sterility, and venereal disease. As Michel Thévoz so appropriately put it: "Injecting the skin with soot-black, the color of bad luck, represents a kind of vaccination against evil spells" (*Le Corps Peint*). Among some peoples, the very pigments used in tattoos are thought to possess magic qualities. The formula for certain pigments apparently includes a woman's milk—preferably from a woman breast-feeding a little girl—thereby transmitting the milk's fortifying virtues to the wearer of the tattoo. Protection reaches its maximum if a verse of the Koran is recited during the operation. In a strange parallel with the "moustache tattoos" on Ainu women in Japan, the term for tattoo used by Moroccan women is *tamart*, which means "beard" or "chin." Among certain Berber tribes, it is also called *tagzzayt*, which signifies "scar" or even "vaccination." As explained by ethnologist Mireille

Henna, applied for ceremonies. Morocco. Agadir province.

Morin-Barde, "it is a woman who does the tattooing—reportedly handed down from mother to daughter—with the help of a needle, making a series of pricks that produce several drops of blood, purportedly making it impure and explaining disapproval. The spot is then rubbed with plants whose juices leave a bluish color. The chin tattoo is usually very simple, just a vertical line between two dotted lines. On the pale skins of Berber women, it is sometimes more lavish with the addition of two feathery, diagonal lines that meet underneath the lower lip; variations on this pattern can also be found on the forehead. The women from a tribe in the Middle Atlas that migrates further south sometimes have a little palm leaf on the forehead, at the base of the eyebrows, which they call *nebla*, "the palm tree" (*Splendeurs du Maroc*, [Tervuren, Belgium: Royal Museum for Central Africa, 1998]).

These modest decorations, obvious vestiges of primitive bodily markings, hardly rival the "baroque" appearance of certain festive ornaments. In the southern Atlas, for instance, drawings done in harqous (a blackish substance obtained by burning various types of organic matter) are used to extend and intensify the tattoo (or even double its effect, according to certain ethnologists). Unlike tribal markings, harqous is just temporary make-up, and thus a tool of seduction. It artificially retraces the eyebrows, which are sometimes plucked completely so that the line can be easily modified. The decorative grammar is in no way improvised, and is dominated by dotted circles, long zigzags down to the

Elegant Moroccan woman perceived through her veil.

chin, and subtle alignments of little crosses, dots, herringbone or v-patterns, all drawn with the aid of a twig. Even more than harqous, designs made with henna have retained a powerful, ceremonial appeal. "It is a plant from Paradise, a blessed, ceremonial plant present at every event, from birth to funeral. Among women, it wards off bad genies, evil spells cast by jealous rivals, and anything that might threaten a woman's happiness. . . . From a medical standpoint, henna seems to have a healing effect on scrapes, burns, pricks, and insect bites. Furthermore, its repeated use hardens the skin and prevents chilblains. For that reason, men also use it" (Odette du Puigaudeau, *Arts et Coutumes des Maures*).

Its original role hardly matters, for in Arab lands henna remains truly sovereign. The name of Allah is written in henna on the forehead of newborns, by way of protection. Henna is used for the flowery arabesques drawn on the palms and backs of a bride's hands, as well as on her feet. Such patterns function simultaneously as finery and talisman, garment and protection. Henna is abetted in its task of beautifying and seducing by its inseparable "cousin," kohl, a makeup found throughout North Africa and the Middle East, whose Arabic name means "black" and "everything that blackens." The prophet Mohammed himself even recommended the use of kohl. It allegedly protects the eyes and favors the growth of eyebrows. Oriental beauties soon realized, of course, that it also intensified their gazes, often the only seductive weapon allowed them underneath their veils.

BODY PAINTING:
ENTER THE SACRED

The Caduveo Indians like to repeat that, "an unpainted body is a dumb body. You must be marked to be a man." As wonderfully described by Claude Lévi-Strauss in *Tristes Tropiques* (Paris: Plon, 1955), this Brazilian people has elevated the art of body painting to rarely attained heights of expressiveness. Nothing is left to chance, however, in their decorations that closely resemble Western playing cards. Ignoring the natural architecture of the face, Caduveo tribes have created a repertoire of extremely complex patterns whose infinite details reflect the diversity of castes and complexity of status. Here a face becomes a blazon; painting functions as writing. Whereas the art of carving wood is reserved to men, that of decorating pottery and skin is the prerogative of women. In the latter sphere, they are undisputed virtuosos, embellishing and elaborating traditional motifs with great inventiveness. According to Lévi-Strauss, several hundred patterns still existed in the 1930s. "Formerly, the patterns were tattooed or painted; only that latter method survives," explained the anthropologist. "With a fine bamboo spatula dipped in sap from the genipap tree—initially colorless but which oxidizes to a blue-black color—the artist improvises on the sitter, using no pattern, sketch, or reference marks. She decorates the upper lip with a motif in the form of an arc with spirals at both ends; then she divides the face with a vertical line, sometimes intersected horizontally. The face thus drawn and quartered—or even carved in diagonal—is then freely decorated with arabesques that pay no attention to the presence of eyes, nose, cheeks, forehead or chin, as though elaborated on a blank surface. These skillful, asymmetrical yet balanced compositions are begun at a given point and carried to the end without hesitation or revision. They rely on relatively simple forms such as spirals, S-shapes, crosses, and Greek key and volute patterns, but these are combined in such a way that every work is original in nature." On seeing this profusion of marks, missionaries displayed alarm at such intolerable contempt for the work of the Creator. "Why are you so dumb?" replied the Caduveo Indians, disgusted by such men whose raw skins barely differentiated them from a state of nature. Yet it must be admitted that these decorative practices no longer respond to the same religious considerations; although the Caduveo continue to adorn their bodies with appealing graphics, they now do so purely for aesthetic pleasure. Once again, the undeniable sensuality of this "art of appearances" should never be underestimated. Lévi-Strauss called it "visual surgery," suggesting that "perhaps never has the erotic effect of makeup been so systematically and consciously exploited." Whereas a curvilinear style is usually adopted for facial painting, a geometric style is used for the body. Beyond these formalist distinctions, however, Caduveo graphic art must ultimately be interpreted, as Lévi-Strauss put it, "as the fantasy of a society which seeks, with unquenched passion, the means to express symbolically the institutions it might have if its interests and superstitions did not get in the way."

Caduveo woman with painted face. Photo by Lévi-Strauss, 1936.

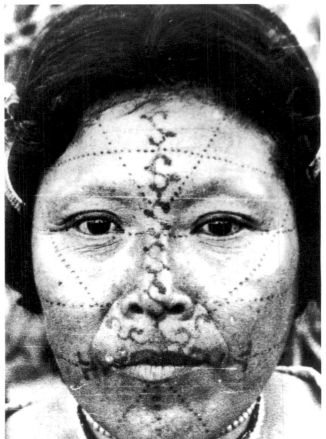

Whatever the formal inventiveness and visual quality of body painting in the eyes of Westerners, such painting is in no way gratuitous. Although the Papua of New Guinea or the Nuba of Sudan may daub their faces and bodies, such acts have nothing in common—despite appearances—with the performances of Yves Klein or other modern practitioners of "Body Art." As Michel Thévoz so rightly put it, body painting constitutes "a regular reminder of roots, like myths and in conformity with myths." The "uncanniness"—to use a Freudian term—of gaudily painted faces suddenly allows bestial forces to surge forth. Divided, shattered, recomposed, the face becomes a series of voids, protuberances, crevices, or orifices. Unlike makeup that aspires to a natural effect, body painting is loud, shameless, sometimes even obscene. It advocates the disintegration of the ego, smashing the respectable façade of appearances. Just as the mask of ancient tragedy was supposed to arouse fright, face painting should render humans unlike themselves; it should dehumanize, depersonalize, literally "deface" them. It facilitates a voyage to the Beyond, transforming men into birds, shamans, or spirits. Its visual vocabulary, then, could hardly be less natural: triangles, circles, and straight lines mask the face, refuting and sometimes outrageously obliterating it. Colors of rare stridency play on contrasts, clashes, ruptures, dissonance. True enough, painting is ephemeral—unlike scarring and tattooing—so its visual impact can be all the more violent. It represents a complete break with everyday life; it is finery for rites or dancing, for weddings and funerals. It also opens the door to prohibited forces of the Beyond, lifts the veil on taboos, heightens awareness of impurity. Among the Kayapo Indians of Brazil, for example, women of marriageable age and wives (whether mothers or not) mutually paint their faces and bodies with linear, longitudinal drawings that evoke, despite superficial appearance, mythical animals from primal ages. In New Guinea, meanwhile, the natives of Mount Hagen transform themselves into "scarecrow warriors" of rare violence: body painting, face ornaments, outfits of feathers, and other accessories all convey the same message of ferocity and virility. Among North American Indians such as the Sioux, a wound itself will be magnified by being ringed with a spectacular red line. Through the grace of decoration, a face may also be transformed into a prayer or plea addressed to heavenly spirits.

(top) Young woman from Zaire. Equator province, on the border with Congo.
(middle) Kikuyu dancer; his body is painted with a mixture of grease and chalk. Central Kenya.
(bottom) Young woman from the Ivory Coast, her body painted for an initiation ceremony.

Thus, the Moqui (Hopi) Indians paint vertical strips on their cheeks in order to bring rain, or diagonal lines to plead for a change in the direction of the wind. Plains Indians such as the Arapaho adorned their foreheads with a semicircle that signified swiftness, alluding to the vast heavens from which lightning falls. Like tattooing and scarification, face painting is here a symbol of bravery, endurance, and combativeness. Whereas the Inuit

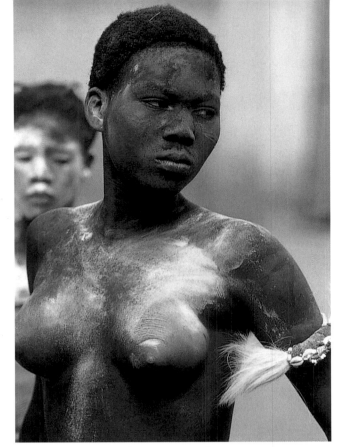

Voodoo ceremony. Abomey.

tattoo their foreheads with the tails of the whales they have killed, great Indian chiefs indicated their exploits and the number of enemies felled by striping their faces and haloing their heads with feathers, turning finery into military arithmetic.

In northern Ghana, men plaster their bodies with white earth and then draw a network of lines on their skin, giving them the startling appearance of walking skeletons. This is perhaps a symbolic way of recalling the permanent dangers surrounding them. In contrast, among the Baining of New Britain, a fine layer of ash mixed with sugar and honey is used to put a shine on the bodies of dancers.

In spite of variations, color symbolism seems to be universal across both time and space. Thus, black often has troubling connotations, associated with the world of darkness and night, a reminder of primordial chaos. Red, the color of blood, is usually associated with fertility and life. White, at the other extreme, represents the color of mourning and purification in many societies.

But sometimes the exuberance of painterly imagination outstrips all conventions. Proof of this can be seen in the graphic feats of the Nuba people, who have been the delight of photographers for several decades now. The youngest members of the tribe must limit themselves to red ocher and simple head ornamentation, whereas the older members sport a brilliant range of colors and highly sophisticated headdresses. As demonstrated by James C. Faris, Nuba body painting is designed to embellish the body rather than mask it or hide its structure through symbolic decoration. Small eyes, when ringed with white earth, appear larger; the tall profile of a giraffe, chosen for its verticality, is natural decoration for a person's back; the roots of the hair will be integrated into the visual composition of the face; every muscle will be highlighted by the glow of oiled skin. Everything works together to render the body sublime, to make its strength and beauty dazzle.

Painting, scarification, coiffures, and jewelry all play off one another, transforming the wearer into a magnificent "living artwork." Here a face might be covered with simple washes of ocher or brown, there a body will sport triangles and circles, symbolizing a universe that seeks to express itself through signs. As in many other African societies, three basic colors come into play: red, white, and black, along with their variants. But they are not used to underscore the different parts of human anatomy or distinguish the features of the face—painting here is a coat that covers, destructuring and effacing all symmetry.

Still another African people has imbued body painting and makeup with its full erotic charge: the Bororo Peul living south of the Sahara. Like many nomads, this tribe produces no sculpture, and therefore expresses all its creativity through jewelry and bodily finery. Once a year, around September or October, the Peul plant their tents in the middle of the desert and prepare to celebrate *gerewol*, a spectacular beauty tournament conducted by the men of the tribe. "The men prepare themselves with great care," explains Christiane Falgayrettes-Leveau. "They spread shea butter on their bodies and hair, which they have separated into several tresses. The fragrance is thought to be an aphrodisiac. Then they paint their faces, divided in two by a yellow stripe down the middle. The skin is decorated with dots or checks and little lines of white, yellow, or black, enhancing the sparkle of eyes and teeth, highlighting forehead and cheekbones. Their lips are perfectly redrawn in dark makeup. After having drunk a stimulating beverage, they don their finest apparel—conical hats decorated with beads and feathers, turbans, necklaces, bracelets, glass trinkets, and amulets to favor victory. Only then do they finally begin, before a circle of elders and women, the showy dances that will last until the following day" (*Corps Sublimes*).

Male finery is here elevated to ritual—the virile body has been raised to the status of artwork.

JEWELRY, AMULETS, TALISMANS

The art of finery is as old as the hills. From the humblest people to the grandest, from nomadic tribes to sedentary populations, men and women have always adorned chests, wrists, and earlobes with the baubles we call jewelry, amulets, and talismans. The finest of these regalia—incarnations of superstition and beliefs, insignia of prestige and glory, indeed devices of seduction—have been relegated by Westerners, alas, to the rank of mere accessories. Whether made of silver or gold, feathers, mother-of-pearl, hair, bone, or pig's teeth, an ethnic jewel should in fact be read as a wonderful ideogram of the habits and customs of peoples for whom it often represents their sole wealth. Sometimes collective memories fade and rituals die out, so that this finery remains the sole reminder of the human propensity to exalt and protect ourselves.

Adornments may invoke blessings, may heal, may appease the gods; they may be of bone, stone, clay, shells, or seeds, or—at a later period—of smelted metals, of porcelain, or of glass beads to be bought and sold. The persistence of practices, along with the eclecticism of forms, is constantly surprising. Techniques born in Neolithic times have miraculously survived the ages. In Mauritania, women continue to pierce shells, string fish bones, polish jasper from the Adrar, and compose necklaces of amazonite. In Melanesia artisans still work with stone-age tools. Patience and time do the rest. Another source of amazement is the similarity of forms and materials employed by civilizations with no contact between them, vastly distant in both time and space. For instance, some Bedouin jewelry looks almost identical to ornaments from the Amerindian world. Feather headdresses worn by Papuans appear to be strangely related to Naga headgear, and so on. Cowry shells, valued for their obvious resemblance to female genitals, have been adopted as finery from Africa to the Hindu Kush. Turquoise, known for its healing and evil-averting virtues, is found in many parts of the world: in Ladakh, woman wear it in their hair; in North America, Hopi, Zuni, and Navajo Indians weave it into their jewelry; Tibetan priests, meanwhile, wear it around the neck like a precious talisman. Yellow amber, which also provides protection from the "evil eye," appeals to Berbers and Mauritanians, to the women of Africa and those of Mongolia. Coral, whose flamboyant color evokes blood, light, and life, is a beneficial substance par excellence. Kabyles—a Berber people living in Algeria and

Tunisia—hang a little rod of coral around the neck of a newborn, while their women don it to increase the milk in their breasts, and men wear it to stimulate their sexual ardor. Among Buddhist peoples of Asia, coral finds its way into rosaries and ornaments for the head, neck, wrists, and fingers. The warm sparkle of carnelian enhances the wedding necklaces of Yemeni brides as well as the heavy jewelry of Tekke nomads (Central Asian horsemen who credit coral with warding off death and preventing bleeding, and therefore wear it to protect themselves from falls and their women from miscarriages). The universal nature of superstitions is matched by a similarity of designs. One obsessive pattern is the spiral: on Berber jewelry, swirls inevitably allude to fertility, the cycles of sun and moon. On Buddhist ornaments, concentric circles symbolize birth and reincarnation. The motif of horns, another recurring design, is found not only in the jewelry of Miao women in China, but also among the Ifugao of the Philippines, the Naga of India and Myanmar (Burma), as well as in Africa and among a few Indian tribes of North America! Whether totemic emblem or clan symbol, the properties of the motif probably evolved from magical and propitiatory to decorative. If any one form is universal, however, it must be the serpent. The slinky silhouette of the snake has made its way into the hollow of Berber bracelets from the Aurès region and reappears in stylized form on African rings.

Fortunately, it turns out that much adornment transcends these generalizations. Melanesian finery is so unexpected, unique, ephemeral, and wild that it often

escapes strict categorization. It is living, organic matter—a simple gust of wind destroys it. The same wind might destroy the feather headdress of an Amazonian Indian in Brazil. Historians, alas, are too often obliged to study permanent ornaments of metal or stone preserved in museums. The public, meanwhile, dreams of removing these objects from their display cases, of seeing them dance once again on a woman's breast, imagining the long trail from the silversmith's hands to the fingers and neck of the person for whom they were made. Nothing could be colder and more fleshless than an orphaned jewel, impaled like a dead butterfly or stuffed animal. It is the job of ethnologists to bring to life the habits and customs that elevated a jewel to the rank of sacred apparel, amulet, or talisman.

Few lands have been as enamored of jewelry, apparently, as North Africa with its numerous ethnic groups. As proof, just stroll through the souks (markets) of Marrakech and Tiznit, or admire the haughty rural women (as opposed to urban ladies) whose heavy pendants glimmer in the sun and tinkle to with each footstep. Yet there is nothing gratuitous about these complex structures in which showiness rivals sacredness. Writing about Berber jewelry in the 1950s, Jean Besancenot noted that, "in the recent past . . . jewelry constituted a mark of clan as surely as tattoos and the patterns of wool blankets worn over the shoulders." Bracelets, diadems, earrings, rings, chains, and necklaces therefore served as a sign of identity and recognition, transcending a purely decorative function. With the possible exception of the cloak-pins known as "fibulas," whose utilitarian purpose is

Berber necklace made of coral, silver, and glass pearls. Morocco.

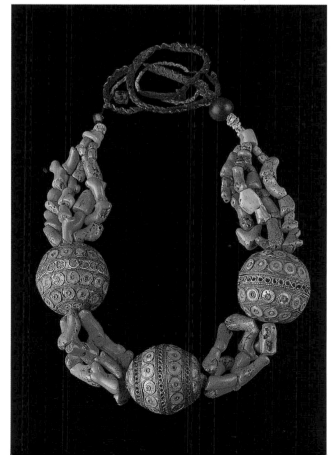

obvious (North African women of today still clasp their garments with these ancient pins), here jewelry is above all a message, a talisman, or even a savings plan! In a region where banks are few and far between, jewelry is easily convertible and therefore constitutes an ideal savings device even as it displays wealth for all to see. During premarital negotiations when a future husband discusses dowry with his fiancée's father, jewels and ornaments figure high on the list, along with cows and goats. The former will remain the sole property of the woman, providing her with material security even in case of divorce. In Algeria, a young Kabyle woman thus receives her jewels at the time of her marriage: diadem, earrings, bracelets, anklets, large fibulas, and necklaces. She will only wear them, however, on her wedding day and for major religious or family celebrations (birth, circumcision, funerals). The rest of the time, Kabyle women wear lighter and more modest jewelry—wearing none at all, however, would be a crime.

And yet the magical, protective nature of such jewelry is usually more important than its material value. Its round or pointed shape, the prophylactic properties of its materials (gemstones, coral, amber, etc.), and its decoration dictate its use in a given ritual. In Great Kabylia, an anklet is attached to the scarf of a young boy at the time of his circumcision; the same type of ornament is placed on one of the feet of a bride during the henna ceremony. Highly protective round fibulas (*tibzimin*) are placed for seven days near the bed of a woman who has just given birth. The most popular amulet, however, is undoubtedly the "hand of Fatima," a pendant or brooch in the shape of a hand. All powers converge in this hand—it is kissed or clasped, is prayed to and implored, can seal pacts, and is used to bless or cast spells. Its five fingers allude to the five pillars of Islam: profession of faith, prayer, alms-giving, fasting during Ramadan, and pilgrimage to Mecca.

Dating back to the most ancient times, cosmogonic designs also possess undeniable powers of protection. The image of the crescent appeared in Mesopotamia in the third millennium B.C.E., incarnating the vital association of sun and moon, fire and water; much later, it became the symbol of Islam. Similarly, the amazing bestiary incorporated into the jewelry of Berber nomads takes its origins from a repertoire that predated Koranic precepts. Ignoring Islamic prohibitions on the depiction of living creatures, these snake heads, ram horns, jackal paws, gazelle hooves, salamander and lizard bodies, fish and turtle shapes adorn bracelets, earrings, broaches, and fibulas. Here again, old fertility rites are being invoked, and the eternal hope for long life is being expressed in a poetic, naïve way. What else do those fresh roses and jasmine convey, what do those pomegranates with their billions of seeds symbolize, if not the terribly human dream of eternal happiness?

In this particular art of beauty and appearance, it is women who prove to be the greatest artists. Devising their finery from elements purchased from the jeweler (beads, coral, rosettes, coins, hands, fish, bells, enamel beads), inspired coquetry spurs them to compose beautiful ornaments in which sophistication rivals whimsy. Employing ancestral tech-

Silver amulet in the shape of Fatima's hand. Morocco.

niques, some women even fashion the pendants for their necklaces, shaping amber paste (known for its medicinal virtues) into a heart, crescent, or star, sometimes including a few cloves for their powerfully aphrodisiac effect. Alas, in North Africa and elsewhere, designs are vanishing and customs are changing, indeed dying out. Gold, although judged impure by the prophet Muhammad, has replaced massive jewelry of silver, a rural metal par excellence. Synthetic beads and plastic imitations can now be found among jewelry whose uniformity sounds the death-knell of the ancient Berber repertoire. And yet, if ethnologist Henriette Caps Fabrer is to be believed, "these jewels, in terms of their technique, massiveness, combination of refinement and Berber coarseness, remain medieval works right in the twentieth century" (Bijoux Berbères d'Algérie, [Edisud, 1990]). Although it rarely leaves the wooden chest where it is now piously preserved, traditional Berber jewelry only assumes its full artistic impact when displayed against shawls of coarse wool or cotton formerly worn by women. Hieratic and powerful, such jewels perhaps represent the last traces of pre-Islamic civilizations, now vanished forever.

Bedouin metalwork, fascinating in many respects, shares with North African jewelry this same baroque profusion of chains, bells, multicolored beads, coins, warm stones such as agate, garnet, carnelian, and amber, and also glass, faience, gold, and copper. As portable merchandise, jewelry has always been viewed by nomadic peoples as a perfect form of saving. It is therefore easy to under-

Moroccan woman adorned for a Moussem festival.

stand why today's Bedouins, influenced by the urban predilection for gold, have succumbed to the economic appeal of the yellow metal over their ancestors' one. Unfortunately, rarity, changes in taste, and the intrinsic value of the stones and precious metals have led to the loss of many valuable items of jewelry. Furthermore, since tradition demands that jewels be destroyed on the death of their owner, age-old styles and patterns are dying out forever. By buying up the rare "survivors" on markets in Riyadh and Jeddah, Western collectors are thereby preserving, in their own way, a heritage in danger of extinction. Among the most extravagant Bedouin finery, it is impossible to overlook the large belts of bells that women wear on festive evenings. Their spectacular size is matched by their sound effect. It is said in Oman that this dancing jewelry is designed to warn a man of a woman's approach. Jewels worn on the head—diadems, side pendants with tiny chains, bells, and gems—also rival one another in splendor and chromatic boldness. Supple and alive, they frame and extend the face in order to exalt it all the better. The same inventiveness can be seen in the use of rings of highly varied styles, which also defy any attempt at classification. Although they play a basically decorative role today, not long ago rings still boasted a powerful talismanic charge. Up to four rings might be worn on the same hand, each with its well-determined place. In the Sultanate of Oman, a set of ten rings—five identical pairs—is still offered to brides, enabling them to display an identical pattern on each finger of both hands. This gift perhaps symbolizes the sealing of two fates. Toe-rings, meanwhile, are almost never seen on the Arabian peninsula, and are allegedly of African origin.

The jewelry worn by Turkmen women, traditionally of solid silver decorated with gilding and carnelian cabochons, can sometimes be mistaken for Arabic metalwork. Like the Bedouins, these former nomadic shepherds (now living in northern Afghanistan, northeastern Iran, and Turkmenia), elevated adornment to the status of artwork. Literally covered from head to toe with dazzling jewelry (diadem, amulets, pendants, and bracelets), a young Turkmen bride shows off the wealth that her father is offering her husband. Veritably "bound" by her magnificently embroidered garments, staggering under a mass of metal (which can attain forty pounds on the wedding day), she is presented to the world as an "idol" smothered by the weight of tradition. It is only after the birth of her first child that a woman will lighten, little by little, her daily ornaments. Once she is no longer of childbearing age, she will never again wear silver ornaments in her hair. One of the most appealing and most widespread items among the Turkmen people is none other a large, heart-shaped, partly fire-gilded amulet. Women wear this symbol of pure and faithful love on their chests or backs, or attach it to their braids. Another typical Turkmen ornament is a round disk richly decorated in openwork patterns, from which slim pendants dangle and tinkle to the rhythm of footsteps. A *tumar*, or "amulet-holder," meanwhile, hangs from the neck by a strap of thick cloth adorned with carnelians and silver plaques; it is triangular, with a small cylindrical case containing a verse of the Koran designed to protect the wearer of this precious talisman. Here again, charms and bells add their aural effects to the visual appeal. The jewelry that best symbolizes the Turkmen women's unbridled enthusiasm for finery, however, is none other than the large, solid bracelets that Tekke women don two at a time, until their arms are covered from wrist to elbow. Rigid as armor plating, without clasps, composed of ten or eleven modules edged with sharp serration, the decoration of these devices of seduction and torture echoes the repertoire of the rich belts worn by men, as well as that of weapons and harnesses. True enough, within the Turkmen hierarchy, women have to compete with horses for the master's interest and for the beauty of their finery.

Heart-shaped Turkmen pendant (silver and cornelian).

In these regions of harsh and even hostile climate, the borderline between jewel and amulet once again seems very slight, as witnessed by the multitude of talismans designed to ward off the evil eye. The simplest ones are sometimes just stitched onto clothing or hats, sometimes hidden under a scarf. Thus the *gupba*, or embroidered caps worn by young Turkmen women prior to marriage, is adorned with little disks, charms, bells, fish, and strings of beads, sometimes even with the feathers of owls, hawks, pheasants, or chickens. If her dowry is not totally paid the day after the wedding, an unfortunate bride will suffer the humiliation of having to wear this premarital hat all her life! Sometimes an amulet is no more than a small silver box filled with plaster or putty, usually worn stitched to the chest, forearm, or underarm—that is where, according to local beliefs, the soul will leave the body at death. Symbolism sometimes harks back to ancient beliefs, as witnessed by a Tekke jewel in the form of the tree of life; called *dagdan*, which means "dawn," it allegedly symbolizes the advent of a new world. Women from southern Tajikistan and Uzbekistan, meanwhile, adorn their foreheads with several dancing rows of small, stamped, silver disks. Their broaches take the form of an openwork medallion, which allegedly constitutes, according to certain specialists, a vestige of an ancient solar cult. In Bukhara, the top of fibulas sport a stylized bird (perhaps a phoenix), while in Khorezm young women wear strange caps of faceted silver adorned with colored stones or glass that sparkle in the light. Their necklaces are stacked in multiple garlands of alternating beads of coral and coins, symbolizing fertility and prosperity

It is nevertheless another central Asian country that has been famous since antiquity for the beauty of its gemstones—Afghanistan. Rubies come from the region of Jagdalek, emeralds from Panshir, topazes from Kandahar, and lapis lazuli—prized since the days of Egyptian pharaohs—from the Sare-Sang mines in Badakhshan. Thanks to these gems, countless jewels have been endowed with timeless

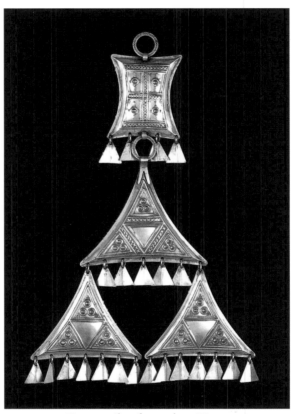

Touareg silver breastplate. Niger.

sparkle. Although Afghan women are today no more than shadows, gliding ghostlike down the devastated streets of Kabul (the *chadri* that covers these "impure" beings from head to toe offers no visible trace of finery), there remains the memory of jewelers' stands at the market, which dazzled the eye back in the days of peace. Armor-like necklaces set with agates, votive broaches, "masked" (i.e., hidden) rings, triangular amulet-holders, and so on, are the repositories of an ancient art of the steppes, and are now the pride of collectors.

Like their North African sisters, women living in the southern Sahara display a passion for jewels and finery. Although silver remains the favorite metal of the Touareg nomads, Peul women from southern Mali are drawn to the glitter of gold—their monumental earrings are hammered into a quatrefoil shape that attains an almost abstract purity. So heavy that they can tear the earlobe, these ostentatious signs of family wealth weigh up to ten or eleven ounces and are supported by a thin cord skillfully hidden in the lady's hair. In contrast to this "modern" appearance that appeals to Western eyes, Senegalese goldsmiths use extensive graining and filigree work and willingly draw inspiration from European models. Wolof women, for example, highly prize broaches of gilded wire in the form of open-winged butterflies or baskets of flowers, revealing the Senegalese artisans' adaptation to their customers' demands. Older items, however, still betray the influence of North African techniques and repertoire as transmitted by

Mauritanian tribes. Among their most original accomplishments are the splendid, weighty pear-shaped ornaments that enhance the complex architecture of headdresses.

Yet more than any other people of West Africa, it is the Akan of Ghana who have elevated gold, with its color and glitter, to cult status. The incorruptible metal, emblem of wealth and power, was so abundant in the area that it once gave its name to the

Akan chief (Ghana) with beads and "wasuman" gold.

region: Ghana was called the "Gold Coast" until its independence in 1957. Akan monarchs were not Muslims, and were therefore not subject to the Koranic injunction against male jewelry—they literally staggered under the weight of their magnificent finery, requiring the help of young servants in order to move around! Women along the coast were also laden with necklaces, bracelets, rings, and chains of gold, copper, and ivory, according to English writer John Lok in 1554. The most detailed description of Akan jewelry nevertheless comes from Jean Barbot, a seventeenth-century French Huguenot and slave trader. The plates illustrating his account reveal an extraordinary repertoire of forms—abstract and geometric ornaments and beads, open-work spirals and disks—which contemporary Ashanti goldsmiths immediately recognize as designs of Akan origin. This frenzy of magnificence and ostentation resurfaces in today's theatrical "gold festivals" that serve as an excuse for incredible displays of family wealth. Under the shimmering sun, all eyes are dazzled by bracelets, necklaces, diadems, fly whisks, and even artificial eyeglasses! Gold remains so venerated in certain regions of West Africa that women

who do not have the means to acquire costly jewelry wear imitations made of straw and wax dipped in a tincture of saffron and henna.

We seem to have come a long way from the ancestral fear of gold—endowed with its own life, able to wound, kill, and drive mad the person who discovered it, the precious metal was thought to grow like a plant, proliferating, and even moving from one place to another. This evil probably long impeded its widespread use.

Whereas in Ghana emphasis was placed on glorifying society's supreme monarch, in the Ivory Coast individual finery apparently held sway. This fundamental difference is probably explained by the absence of chieftaincies among the coastal peoples. Thus, the gold rings that constituted one of the pinnacles of Akan art (if only for the moral message they conveyed to the person who gazed upon them) were practically nonexistent among the Baule people who, on the other hand, excelled in the art of lost-wax casting, thereby creating an infinite variety of gold beads and spiral disks of spidery finesse, sometimes topped by the profile of a bird, fish, or crocodile. Men and women also adorn their hair or necks with little "pendant masks" that can attain extreme elegance. They are perhaps "portraits" of friends or lovers, ancestors or deceased kings, but the Baule simply call them "human heads."

More than just a sign of social prestige, an item of jewelry actively protects the wearer. Better still, it is endowed with veritable autonomy, marking the boundary between two realms: the physical and the spiritual. Thanks to jewelry, each part of the human body acquires strong visual value, imbued with social and religious symbolism, even as it conveys an undeniable erotic charge. The large bronze ornaments handed down from generation to generation by the Fang people thus stress the musculature of arm or leg, or the daintiness of ankle or wrist. Among the Dan people on the Ivory Coast, heavy anklets feature bells that mark the rhythm of dances; among the Ibo of Nigeria, meanwhile, anklets are so large that they become instruments of alienation by obliging the women who wear them to walk with their legs spread apart, yet they are still greatly coveted by women of high standing. These anklets, made by a blacksmith who himself attaches them to the ankles of young women, are hammered from a fine copper alloy and symbolize the plenitude of the sun through their geometric pattern and shape.

Ivory, another royal substance considered indestructible, obviously alludes to the strength of elephants. Among the Bamileke people of Cameroon, "the chiefs traditionally appropriate the tusks of all elephants killed," according to Pierre Harter, thereby "maintaining a monopoly on the ivory trade. . . . Items in ivory thus became the exclusive attributes of royal dignitaries and fon." Bamum chiefs also wore magnificent bracelets whose pure lines underscored the shapely curve of an arm. Whether carved from a hippopotamus tooth or elephant tusk, these highly rare items from Eastern Africa reveal the profound aesthetic concerns of people who never created sculptures or masks. Yet Africans perhaps display the most inventiveness and talent when it comes to their

unbridled love of beads. Who has never seen the wonderful beaded jewelry of Zulu tribes? Made solely by the women, these costly ornaments are worn only during ritual ceremonies such as the initiation of young girls, weddings, and the commemoration of ancestors. Patterns and arrangements of colors are far from arbitrary, since they reveal the wearer's rank and the context in which the finery is worn—as a sign of love or affection, of conjugal or filial respect, and so on. Photographer Angela Fisher has documented over forty patterns among Masai tribes alone. For the Dinka, every row of beads worn by a groom on his wedding day indicates the number of head of livestock he owns.

Halfway between garment and jewel, many accessories underscore differences in sex or status. In northern Tanzania, an extraordinary metal gorget (or neck-piece) marks a woman as the wife of an important personage. In Cameroon, the metallic loincloth worn by Kirdi women, composed of series of interlocking little strips of wrought iron, stresses the pubic area more than it hides it. Similarly, the buttock coverings worn by Mongo women are decorated with large and thoroughly titillating raffia pompoms! Those worn by Mangbetu women, meanwhile, are woven of banana leaves in geometric patterns that irresistibly attract the eye; few other ethnic groups have elevated accessories and finery to such heights as can be seen in their extraordinary headdresses woven from reeds, designed as a veritable extension of the skull. Like an item of jewelry, hair can be a sign of rank or instrument of beauty. As Christiane Falgayrette-Leveau aptly put it, "in almost all

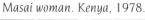

Masai woman. Kenya, 1978.

traditional societies of black Africa, the coiffure is the medium for a language as subtle and multifarious as the countless ways of dressing and adorning oneself. . . . Extremely complex codes are engaged and sustained, depending on whether the hair is left unbound and never cut, partially or totally shaved, scented, oiled, covered in kaolin or red ocher, plastered with earth or mud, braided or pulled into a bun, enhanced with the addition of hairpieces, feathers, cowries, combs or pins" (*Corps Sublimes*). Among the Baule people, for instance, shaving the skull indicates the passage from one state to another (usually widowhood). For many peoples, young women must reach marriageable age before they can put combs and pins in their hair as tangible signs of their entry into society. The hairstyles of today's black women are equally fascinating in their diversity—twisted into serpentine locks, divided into checkerboard patterns, or flattened like a heavy watermelon about to burst. The respectful lens of photographer Okhai Ojeikere has captured, documented, and archived no fewer than one thousand hairstyles in the past thirty years! A lock of hair can be a glowing earthworm, a sensual swirl, an obedient shell, a falsely rebellious hank; it can be crinkled, smooth, taut, slack, curled, frizzed, opaque, shiny, as natural as it is artificial. Usually flirting with abstraction, the skull thereby becomes an ideal medium for "temporary sculptures" of hair and synthetic or silken tresses. Created by the skilled hands of hairdressers in the ancient kingdom of Dahomey, amazing "ornamental hairstyles" attained heights of virtuosity that would be the envy of every beautiful lady today.

In Africa, however, men are not excluded from the competitive game of beauty and appearance. Feathers, leaves, grasses, and shells as well as barkcloth, metal, and beads all go into headwear whose symbolic richness is matched by its stylistic eclecticism, from the Fang's mask-headdresses to the Luba's beaded headgear to the raffia hats found in the Congo. Here again, each material indicates a different rank or status. Animal fur, claws, and horns seem to hark back to ancient beliefs even as they valorize courage and virility—they should perhaps be seen as phallic substitutes or as distant reminders of some trophy. Once a haughty hunting garment, headdresses are today often relegated to the role of accessory or museum item.

When it comes to sacred objects, India may be the only continent

(*top*) M'Huila virgin. Angola.
(*middle*) Nyangatom shepherdess. Ethiopia, Gemu Gofa province, Nakua.
(*bottom*) Young girl after puberty rites. Angola, Huila province.

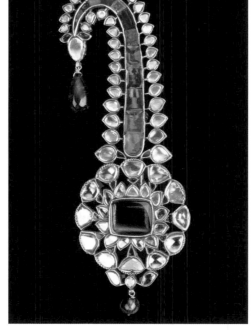

Indian bride from Rajasthan.   17th-century jigha from Mughal.   Sardar Singh, maharajah of Jodhpur, 1902.

that can rival Africa. In India, both men and women, whatever their religion, mark the different stages of their lives through countless ceremonies during which their finery is invested with powerful symbolism. Items of jewelry are talismans of fertility as well as marks of prosperity, thus transmitting a message even as they wordlessly announce the status of the wearer. As incarnations of the power of gods and goddesses, jewels admirably convey the wealth and complexity of religions and the profundity of certain philosophical concepts. The importance of jewelry on the Indian continent is justified by sacred literature, since the Vedic texts grant it symbolic virtues. The gods and goddesses also wear gems as attributes of their power: long before rajas and emperors, Vishnu wore sapphires, Indra wore rubies, Agni wore diamonds. Nor is it rare to see bodhisattvas (future buddhas) stagger under the

weight of a gilded tiara or diadem of highly sophisticated metalwork. As to nymphs and goddesses, their sensuous curves drip with necklaces and pendants, as seen on the wall paintings at Ajanta and the bas-reliefs at Khajuraho.

At a very early date, scholarly treatises dealt with jewelry and how to make it—a Sanskrit text from the third century C.E. described in full detail not only the way to work gold, but also all the laws governing its trade. Indian jewelry truly blossomed once Muslims arrived on the subcontinent. Few monarchs in the world cultivated such a passion for costly gems as the Mughal emperors, who elevated precious gemstones into a veritable cult, associating them with beauty, wealth, and power. The great Akbar is said to have had no fewer than three treasurers just to superintend his jewelry, while his successor Jahangir boasted six fortresses to hold all his valuables. This passion for appearances was then adopted by the maharajas, who wore strings of pearls and heavy gems as tangible signs of their opulence. Among the gems most prized by Indian monarchs were emeralds, which, apart from their intrinsic beauty, were credited with therapeutic and talismanic properties, notably the ability to counteract the effects of poison. Portuguese merchants established at Goa on the Indian coast regularly supplied the Mughal court with gemstones of all kinds—rubies, sapphires, amethysts, and so on. Workshops in Jaipur and Gujurat would engrave them with floral and foliate patterns—or else with prayers and religious verses supposed to increase their talismanic properties—and these magnificent gems would then be mounted on aigrettes and other ornaments for turbans (the emblem of royal power), as well as bracelets, necklaces, and—more frequently—pendants that hung from a string of pearls. Mughal rulers also launched the fashion for enameling; they had bracelets, necklaces, and even belt buckles enameled in myriad colors, like a miniature echo of the wonderful floral compositions of semi-precious stones set into their white marble palaces.

Far—very far—from this princely magnificence, today's Indians deploy limitless imagination in their finery. Thus even when performing the most thankless tasks, the forearms of a female peasant in Gujurat or Rajasthan will tinkle to the sound of multiple bracelets. Plastic has often replaced ivory, of course, and glass has supplanted enamel here as elsewhere. But it hardly matters: all women in India, right from infancy, are appar-

eled like goddesses. Jewelry constitutes a woman's sole wealth, for that matter, the only goods she legally owns. Although primarily expressing an Indian woman's grace and sensuality, jewelry also indicates her marital status. Thus in Tamil Nadu, a bride wears a necklace whose form and decoration constitute symbols indicating the caste and religious sect of the wearer. The little crab-claw pendants on a "tali" necklace are a sign that its owner probably belongs to the Chettiar caste of coastal traders in southern India. Some ornaments reach surprising length, and are displayed only on the wedding day or "sixtieth birthday" (a particularly auspicious day). Although the decorative repertoire is essentially based on nature—as demonstrated by strings of evil-averting amulets in the shape of flowers, fruit, and vegetables supposed to increase fertility—sometimes the visual idiom can be more abstract or geometric, even attaining "cubist" tones of surprising modernity. Take, for example, earrings and bracelets from the Madurai area, with their "art deco" look—which in fact is a geometric transcription of prayers and incantations known as yantras. Yet what most surprises and perhaps appeals to Western eyes is certainly the natural, constant elegance of Indian women, whatever their wealth or rank. Their arms and forearms are laden with a multitude of bracelets of glass, ivory, or bronze, their ankles are weighted with heavy bands of silver (in Rajasthan), their noses flaunt a little stone and their toes sport rings—everything is designed to attract a man's gaze, to incarnate a woman's constant sacredness. Sometimes, sure enough, this profusion of

Peasant from the Jodhpur region, 1996.

Karo woman wearing Padaung silver earrings. Indonesia.

jewelry masks a much more prosaic goal, namely hoarding wealth for a rainy day.

India can also show itself to be tribal and warrior-like, as illustrated by the striking finery worn by the Naga, a people of Mongol stock living on the borders of China and Myanmar (Burma). These dreaded headhunters wear jewelry of rare beauty: necklaces of carnelian beads or shells of pharaonic appearance, copper bracelets, bronze torques (twisted bands), and sophisticated bead ornaments from which little bronze bells dangle. Everything proclaims, in ostentatious fashion, the warrior's rank and valor. Although the symbolic language (of colors and rows of circles, squares, and stars) has not yet been fully deciphered, one obsessive iconographic motif stands out: the trophy head. The motif of a pair of buffalo horns, meanwhile, tattooed on warriors' chests in a stylized "V" form, is also found engraved on the shell earrings which only the most experienced headhunters are entitled to wear.

Due to extreme poverty, some tribes from northern Thailand (Karen, Hmong or Meo, Akha, Lahu, Yao, and Lisu peoples) have felt obliged to sell the jewelry that once indicated their wealth and social status. They initially melted down the jewels, until they realized that collectors were inclined to pay a price greater than the simple value of the precious metal. Their jewelry includes admirably simple torques of hammered silver worn by men, women, and children alike.

A more "baroque" effect is produced by Himalayan jewelry that clusters on garments like so many talismans designed to ward off evil influences. It is the Newar bronzesmiths and goldsmiths of the valley of Kathmandu who spread this virtuoso metalwork from village to village, transmitting their refined aesthetic to the very ends of China and Mongolia. Here turquoise rules, a symbol of the purity of the celestial universe, along with coral, which endows women with strength and happiness and favors menstruation. Himalayan peoples perhaps display the most inspiration in their head finery. In Ladakh,

Headdress of married Man Taï Pan (Man Coo) woman. Tonkin, Lao Kay province, 1923.

women wear heavy headdresses whose oblong shape is supposed to represent a raised cobra swelling its neck into a hood. This highly symbolic head-wear combines the blue of the sky (through the use of turquoise) with the red of fire (a piece of cloth), even as its weds the woman's natural hair to an animal's fur (the astrakhan ear-pieces), thereby accomplishing a fusion of complementary energies. Apart from the little kingdoms of Java and Bali, which were heavily influenced by India, the peoples of Southeast Asia's archipelagos perpetuated their own artistic and religious traditions through two forms of finery—ritual jewelry on the one hand, and ceremonial fabrics on the other. In Indonesia, Malaysia, and the northern Philippines, these precious ornaments represent domestic wealth as handed down from generation to generation, thus

scrupulously reflecting the owner's social position. The play of shapes, colors, and patterns also expresses, in an extremely codified way, family ties and relationships as well as myths and rituals. Jewelry and fabrics are exchanged during wedding ceremonies, and are an integral part of the economic system of trade between tribes, ethnic groups and, more generally, between coastal populations and inland peoples. Hence, nothing could be less arbitrary or pointless than this finery from the southern hemisphere. Traditional cloths from Sumba, Flores, and Sumatra, like earrings, chest ornaments, and diadems from Sulawesi and Nias, are just modest representatives of a vast universe peopled with symbols and rites (such as body painting, tattooing, and even the filing of teeth). "Should they disappear," worries Swiss collector Jean-Paul Barbier with some justification, "then the entire history of a people with no written annals will vanish." All these gems of metal or cloth represent a complex system of communication accessible only to the initiated, indicating not only rank and status, but also, and above all, an irrevocable development in the course of a lifetime: the transition to adulthood for both men and women, marriage, pregnancy, and preparation for the grand journey to the "otherworld." And yet here as elsewhere, the primary role of finery remains the obvious display of wealth to the rest of the community. During traditional Batak weddings, for instance, the future couple must dress like a princely raja and his wife. The groom wears a sarong woven with metallic threads, and dons a black hat that strongly resembles a derby. On Sumatra, the lucky man sports armbands above the elbow and is dressed in a magnificent red and black cloth called an "ulos." The bride arrives in even more sophisticated garb, her torso draped in dark red scarves that criss-cross (possibly to ward off evil influences), her wrists laden with bracelets, her fingers lengthened with false nails of gold, all of which appear insignificant compared to her extravagant wedding headdress. Composed of a series of thin gold disks hanging from slender needles, this "baroque" headpiece is more than a piece of finery. It is supposed to convey a number of moral maxims to guide the new bride in her married life; the pendants dangling on her forehead, for example, prevent her from looking left or right, a skillful way of indicating that she should henceforth direct her gaze modestly toward the ground. Steeped with *sahala* (magic power), this precious headdress will soon be placed in the protective darkness of the family treasure chest. Only on rare occasions, such as the sacrifice of a water buffalo, will it be allowed to see the light of day again.

Apart from their ostentatious nature and moral function, items of jewelry from the Southeast Asian isles functioned until recently as indispensable objects of mediation between social groups, between the sexes, indeed between different parts of the cosmos. In the highly regimented context of matrimonial exchange, for instance, the "givers of the bride" offered "feminine" cloths to the "takers of the bride," who, in return, handed over "masculine" metal in the form of precious ornaments. These days, this prenuptial "barter" has transcended the framework of ritual exchange and has "wed" itself to the international art market—

Young Kalinga woman from northern Luçon Island, wearing mother-of-pearl earrings.

much age-old finery has thus found its way into the display cases of collectors and museums. And yet for the Sadang and Toraja peoples, a mythical connection is still perceived between the work of a blacksmith today, the primal origins of metal-forging, and the creation of the humanity. You would therefore be ill-advised to handle lightly the precious ornaments found in their imposing houses of carved wood. But for how much longer? No one knows.

Because noble families on northern Luzon, on Sulawesi, and on most eastern Indonesian islands awarded themselves the exclusive privilege of owning and wearing jewelry of gold, less fortunate classes had to make do with transient finery of shells, feathers, and bones. The rudimentary nature of these items was nevertheless transcended by extraordinary inventiveness. In the Philippines, a *sipatal* is a spectacular ceremonial necklace composed of several layers of mother-of-pearl pendants. A *bontoc* takes the form of a headband made of glass beads or snake bones. Young bachelors, meanwhile, sport amazing wickerwork hats decorated with shells in the form of testicles or butterfly wings. The same love of nature and same intimate link between the animal and plant worlds can be detected in finery worn on the Oceanian archipelago. The rule here is exuberance, ardor, and virile strength. In Irian Jaya, Asmat men wear an entire skull as a chest ornament, while warriors from Maprik stick the tusks of wild pigs through their noses. Multicolored feathers, seeds, shells, roots of orchids, palm leaves, human hair, and the teeth of boar, whales or dolphins are

appropriated by Oceanic artists with astonishing ingeniousness in a constant search for the greatest visual impact. The surprising effects are inevitably accompanied by an impression of mobility—whether of rattan, wicker, feathers, or fur, Melanesian ornaments float lightly on the head or down the backs of dancers whose painted bodies and faces further increase the theatrical effect. In Polynesia, garments and finery reflect the degree of sacredness, rank, and wealth of the wearer, as well as testifying to the virtuosity of the artisans who produced them. Materials expected to last because they are rare or sacred (red feathers of the tropic bird, hairs taken from ancestors or enemies, nephrite, sperm-whale bone, tortoiseshell, etc.) contrast with transient materials derived from flowers or seeds. Animal and human teeth are introduced into the composition of necklaces, bracelets, and ornaments for head and chest; coco fibers are used in making flywhisks, combs, and belts. Dangling jadeite earrings worn by Maoris of New Zealand, meanwhile, are endlessly polished with quartz sand, reaching a level of abstraction and formal perfection that almost masks their original function: to store *mana*, the spiritual energy of all those who previously wore them. Kap-kap pendants of seashell and tortoiseshell, worn exclusively by men in New Ireland, are also handed down from generation to generation. Their beauty is rivaled only by the virtuosity of their execution. Few peoples have displayed such an absolute love of mother-of-pearl: reddish and orange nacre is prized for rainbow reflections, green nacre is reserved for ceremonial ornaments, while white

Fijian man wearing a necklace made of sperm whale teeth, c. 1880.

nacre is thought to make the wearer appear more frightening. All this mother-of-pearl is haggled over in "gift-giving contests" similar to the potlatch practiced by North American Indians.

The ever-fascinating mother-of-pearl can also be found thousands of miles away, on loincloths worn by aborigines in Australia, as well as on the magnificent combs stuck in the sophisticated coiffures of Japanese courtesans. In some places, it is used as material for sorcery (its geometric strata symbolizing rain), in others it is a very feminine and sensual substance with beneficial virtues (supposed to protect brides and bring them happiness).

This overview of ethnic beauty would not be complete without a discussion of the Amerindian world, that land of metamorphosis. If feathers were regal among the Papua of Oceania, they were positively imperial among the indigenous peoples of the Americas, north and south. Alas, so much fragile, multicolored finery has vanished into the nether-

world of oblivion, taking entire chapters of the region's history with it. So much metalwork was melted by conquistadors hungry for wealth and power—gold honored by Amerindians as "the sweat of the Sun," silver venerated like "the tears of the Moon." Chest ornaments, diadems, necklaces, and lip plugs—shut away in museum display cases these days—praised the now-defunct power of those half-jaguar, half-bird gods mentioned in the chronicles, of those shamans with their magic potions that once provoked intoxicating trances.

There are, fortunately, ethnic groups who still retain a constant, virgin desire to grasp beauty and make a show of it, thanks to—and via—finery. Largely isolated from the outside world, tribes of Amazonian Indians have for centuries been making ornaments that would turn the world's grand fashion designers green with envy! Here again, nothing is arbitrarily decorative: the feather pendants dangling from the ears of the Kayapo people allegedly improve their

Asparoke Indian chief. Photo by Edward W. Curtis, 1908.

Brazilian wearing a feathered traveling headdress.

hearing and stimulate their intelligence. Every seed or fiber—and especially every feather—woven into a diadem, necklace, or armband conveys some information, indicating age or clan or revealing rank or status.

Similarly, the magnificent feather headdresses worn by the great Indian chiefs photographed by Edward S. Curtis indicated the number of enemies slain, virile strength, and valor in combat. A warrior pictured himself as an eagle, a medicine-man became a thunderbird. Although finery was usually connected to ritual practices (making contact with totemic animals or guardian spirits, acquiring the status of initiate or shaman, establishing a state of purification or healing), it was above all a mark of sexual difference. Given their undeniable erotic charge, jewelry and garments enhance the beauty of the body even as they underscore differences. Bear claws or hawk talons intensify virility; flowers and scented plants glorify sensuality. Young Comanches thus wore all kinds of baubles in their hair, braiding their locks with thin strips of leather decorated with glass breads and brass wire. When they wanted to court a young lady, the braves would top this impressive outfit with a feather headdress, then don necklaces made of wild cat claws, wolves' teeth, and coyote tails. Their clothing shimmered with metallic crosses and crescents. No less inventive when it came to seduction, the Mandan wore mirrors on their wrists and adorned their ears with a variety of tiny beads of glass, iron, shell, and brass. The Plains Indians were probably the most talented when it came to combining colors and materials. Coins, mirrors, ribbons, beads, and sometimes even shoe buttons, medals, and bells went into ornaments that rivaled one another in boldness and artistry.

Amerindian metalworking has never stopped evolving, in fact. Far from being purely negative, the encounter between Europeans and native Americans turned out to be extremely fertile in terms of creativity, as demonstrated by the indigenous finery made with imported beads and the turquoise-studded broaches and belt buckles in the form of Spanish crosses. The irony is that this hybrid jewelry is now sought less by collectors than by tourists—turquoise, the "stone of heaven," allegedly brings good luck and health.

Much more original is the silver jewelry made by the Mapuche people of Chile. Its timeless purity is mesmerizing. Made by men (being their sole craft activity), these earring and pendants are only worn on grand occasions. Yet once a year, women polish their *tupus*—large round fibulas, full like the moon—which they clasp, as their ancestors did, to their magnificent garments.

DRESS:
FROM RITUAL TO SEX APPEAL

"To be naked is to be speechless," say the Dogon people of Mali. Among ethnic African societies that have no written language, garments constitute a symbolic vocabulary alongside scarification and jewelry. A simple string knotted around the waist may carry the same importance as an entire outfit—by demarcating the body's transitional zone, it places bestiality at one remove. Since long before the arrival of woven textiles, African belles have had "wardrobes" composed of the most varied materials. In northern Cameroon, women from Upper Bénoué wear garlands of calabashes as a type of skirt; young Bassari dancers from Guinea adorn their pubic area with metallic ornaments that tinkle to the rhythm of the choreographic movements; Mangbetu women from Zaire cover their buttocks with a garment of black and white fibers woven into so many coded messages.

Under the influence of Islam, however, finery, weapons, and textiles soon became the crucial signs by which members of the noble classes distinguished themselves from their subjects. Arab traveler Al Bakri, visiting the kingdom of Ghana in the eleventh century, described the court's sartorial protocol in these terms: "Among people of the king's religion, only the king and crown prince can wear tailored garments. . . . Whereas all the others wear loincloths of cotton, silk, or brocade . . . the king dons high pointed hats set with

Mangbetu women (woven fiber garment). Zaire.

gold, around which he rolls a turban of very fine cotton." Two centuries later, Ibn Battutah criticized the lack of enthusiasm of Malian peoples to dress in fabrics. "Female servants, slaves, and little girls appear completely naked before men," complained the alarmed traveler, a good Muslim, on seeing these creatures go around unveiled, "breast uncovered." Fabrics soon evolved from simple finery to a unit of exchange along with cowry shells from the Pacific, beads, and spearheads, for fabrics were a most obvious sign of wealth in societies where only the few were granted the prerogative of putting them on.

Although Africans never really abandoned plant and organic substances (dried fruit, bird feathers, shells, animal skins, etc.), they subsequently fell in love with textiles. From birth to death, fabrics orchestrate and mark the stages of the life cycle. In many cases, they even seem to be "as an extension of the human being," in Michèle Coquet's apt phrase in *Textiles Africains* (Paris: Adam Biro, 1993). She was referring to the indigo-dyed cotton fabrics so valued by the famous "blue men," the Touaregs of the Sahara Desert. Penetrating the pores of the skin to the point of imparting a bluish tinge to the wearer,

the garment becomes "finery which clings, transforms, and perfumes the body."

Thus in African lands nothing could be more intimate or personal than dress. The Bambara of Mali hold a family ceremony to celebrate the wearing of the first garment, while in West Africa, newborns are given a cotton thread to mark the fragile connection henceforth linking them to the world of human beings. The Bambara also have an extremely codified use of bogolan loincloths, which are dyed with blackish mud and worn during special occasions when blood is shed. Among men, this means during the hunt or masked rituals; among women, it occurs during excision, an operation perceived as a sacrifice and religious offering to restore a lost order. A new loincloth, called basiae (from *basi*, "blood"), replaces the white cotton one which girded her loins until then, and will henceforth accompany her at each stage of life in which the loss of blood is involved (the consummation of marriage, the birth of each child, etc.). This long cloth with its designs of earth becomes the veritable "shroud" of a woman's life, and will follow her to her grave.

Indeed, in Africa more than any other continent, people like their dead to leave for the next world totally wrapped in fabrics. Among the Kuba of Zaire, the deceased take with them an impressive quantity of the famous raffia fabrics embroidered by women. For a member of this tribe, being buried with European fabrics would be like departing completely naked! In African eyes, woven materials may function as an offering to the gods, a prophetic tool, or a prophylactic measure, so that their decorative and ornamental features seem almost secondary. Far from being purely aesthetic, the shimmering palette of fabrics once again reflects a highly complex set of codes. The white of cotton is often perceived as a primal color, worn in Sudan as sign of light and purity; black represents water, vegetation, darkness; red ocher is associated with blood and sun, yellow ocher with change and transformation. Alternating bands of colors can even constitute a distinct language. On the fabrics worn by Ashanti monarchs, the patterns in the weft act as so many clan emblems or blazons. Dogon priests, when they preside over planting ceremonies, don a cloak of black and white squares that mimic the fields plowed by human hands: the white squares symbolize the white and fertile soil of the plain, the black squares the dry and arid earth of the plateau. Under the influence of Islam, African garments also began acquiring graceful arabesques—inscriptions of the names of Allah, verses from the Koran, magic squares, and designs descended from the ancient Eastern cabalistic tradition (pentagrams, eight-pointed stars, etc.). These snatches of sacred texts are designed to bring health, protection, and happiness to the wearer.

Embroidery is another realm in which Arab iconography has come into its own. It covers not only robes of silk and cotton but also the trousers and hats worn by the Muslim leaders of African societies. The art of embroidery is taught by Koranic masters who are expert in calligraphy. Held in great esteem by the people, embroiderers—all of whom are men—belong to the literate, learned population. The wisest and most skillful of them win the prerogative of embroidering headgear, the head being the most important part of the body according to Islam, because it rises toward heaven and God. But as Islamic weavers began moving around, the old Berber decorative repertoire also began to circulate through African lands. Its chromatic combinations of white, black, rust, and yellow ocher began spreading across Peul fabrics in northern Mali, as did Berber triangle and diamond patterns. A radically different conception can be seen in the long raffia loincloths woven by Kuba women, which introduce disorder into harmony, eliminating any threat of tedious symmetry: diamonds, squares, circles, and rectilinear shapes obey no grid, playing on a sense of void and solid with a rather unique sense of freedom for African art. But the prize for inventiveness certainly goes to the

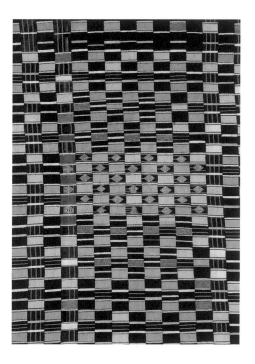

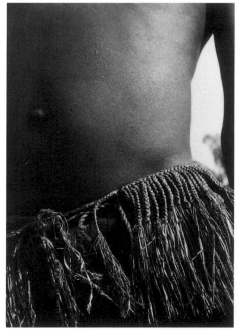

(*top*) Woven cotton loincloth. Ghana, Ashanti kingdom.
(*middle*) Young Akha pygmy woman. Central African Republic, Lobaye region.
(*bottom*) Pygmy bark loincloth. Central African Republic.

beaten barkcloth made by people in Zaire. The Bambuti Pygmies are so known for the quality of their work that they receive orders from neighboring peoples, and have devised a fanciful graphic system that few Western designers can match—stripes in parallel or with no apparent order, barbed or dotted lines, spirals, scrolls, arabesques, curls, stars, suns, grids, vague blotches, and footprints all trace unlikely paths across the cloth. Interwoven vines, spiderwebs, and panther spots are other remote allusions that also indicate the ancient origins of this highly poetic visual art.

As Michèle Coquet rightly stresses, "each piece of bark is conceived as a whole, comparable to a painter's canvas. . . . The loincloths are always made with someone in mind, for whom the patterns will be designed, while each work is unique because the composition is reconceived every time, as is the type of line and design." In short, we seem to be dealing here with unacknowledged haute couture. Drawn toward innovation and a constant questioning of their own decorative principles, Bambuti Pygmies nevertheless

Fully veiled woman. Morocco.

incorporate the most ancient and sacred concerns of their people—thus the same scrolls appear on the surface of cloths and on the skin of humans. the juice from the same gardenia fruit produces black lines on both body and bark. From skin to garment, we seem to have come full circle.

Obviously, in Africa, as well as in many other places on the planet, traditional cloths are encountering severe competition from Western industrial garments. Synthetic dyes are replacing ancient pigments; ritual finery is giving way to the new dictates of fashion. Modern African dress henceforth combines draped cloths with stitched garments. Far from vanishing, however, its extraordinarily creative potential is rebounding from this avalanche of new imagery freed of all symbolism. Western fashion designers make no mistake when they borrow, from here and there, a given pattern or palette or even attitude. There is now a long list of inspired "plagiarists" from Yves Saint Laurent and John Galliano to the young Malian designer Xuly-Bêt.

In some regions, people show, emphasize, reveal; in others, they hide, disguise, obliterate. Dress can be armor and protection; it can become wall and prison. Islam makes no distinction between religious and secular clothing; the way to dress scrupulously follows the prophet's example. In a society that sees itself above all as a "community," morality imposes particularly strict rules of seemliness: hair, bodily hygiene, and clothing are highly codified for both men and women. Men, for instance, are obliged to wear full and flowing garments that hide the body even as they facilitate ablutions and worship (bowing and prostrating in prayer). Most of the time, the garments of Arab origin known as *jellaba*, *kamiss* (tunic), and *abaya* (long cape of cotton or wool) cover everything except face, hands, and feet. Moreover, like all Semitic peoples, Muslims are expected to cover their heads at all times—especially when in a mosque—out of respect for God. This head wear varies from country to country, from simple skullcap to elaborate turban, head scarf, or embroidered hat. Another "Eastern" symbol is the long, bushy beard flowing down the neck, strictly respecting the prophet's instructions to his disciples and all believers to wear one. This face hair, trimmed and maintained according to extremely precise rules, now incarnates not only virile maturity and respectability, but also extreme piety. Indeed, from Iran to Afghanistan, this beard has now become a grim political symbol.

Like many other societies, the Muslim world has assigned highly codified meanings to certain colors. Green, the color primarily associated with Islam, symbolizes hope and life. It can be seen on the bindings of the Koran and on the domes of mosques and shrines, and is also the color of the elect in heaven. Black, more ambivalent, inspires both fear and respect; it is the color of mourning for Shi'ites, but the heroic color of revolution among the descendants of Abbassid rebels, while in today's Iran a sepulchral black cloud envelopes the mullahs' capes and the women's chadors. Similarly, white is associated not only with the death shroud, but also with the pilgrimage that is the high point of every believer's life. More prosaically, white is also the favored color in hot countries. Whereas red is once again the color of passion, blue is associated with the "evil eye." Yellow remains an attribute of power and royalty.

One "accessory" alone sums up the severity of dress habits in Islamic lands—the veil and its various incarnations. If certain commentators are to be believed, the Koran allegedly instructed the prophet's wives to veil themselves, while women in general were to "show their charms" only to their nearest male relatives—father, husband, brothers. "Good" Muslim women must therefore cover their bodies, necks, ankles, and even arms. No legislation, therefore, explicitly insists that they veil themselves completely. Initially, veiling the face was not part of local customs (adat)—it was not practiced by Berbers, Africans, and Southeast Asians. It first became widespread among city dwellers during the Abbassid period, whereas rural women continued to wear a simple headscarf. Nothing could be more complex than this feature of dress, however. The headscarf is perceived by Western women as an absolute symbol of the alienation of their Muslim sisters, yet a certain number of Oriental women see it as an expression of relative modernity. Sure enough, by framing the face and hiding the hair, a hijab offers a guarantee of anonymity: women can go out, work, and occupy a social space formerly confiscated by men. Even better, it becomes sign of respectability, conveying an image of Islamic women in stark contrast to Western depravity. More drastic than the hijab is the black chador in Iran, not to mention the chadri in Afghanistan which provides only a tiny, barred slit—the burqa, or "barrier"—through which a woman can peer: garment as alienation, veil as negation. It would nevertheless be a mistake to present only this coercive, austere image of Islamic dress. In certain North African countries such as Tunisia, traditional marriages offer an opportunity to display finery of rare richness to all and sundry. Even before donning her ceremonial garb, a future bride is the object of every attention: ritual application of henna to hands, feet, and forearms, long preparation of hair (dyed black, braided, and scented), skin completely depilated, washed, purified. It is somewhat as though the body of the bride is shedding its natural state in order to enter a cultivated one, like the culinary process that transforms raw food into cooked dishes. Tunisian matrons will even comment on how "hot" the bride is when they hug her; men, meanwhile, will say that she is "cooked" or "ready for eating." Dressed like a goddess, displayed like an idol, a bride staggers under layers of garments (blouses, tunics, waistcoats, pants, cloaks) comprising specific outfits for the various days of the ceremony. Once again, the patterns seen on embroidery and jewelry are not the product of chance—all are imbued with profound meaning, intimately combining superstition with a love of beauty. A fishbone sewn into a headdress will make the marriage fertile, while a "hand of Fatima" embroidered on a vest will ward off the evil eye. Shawls and

Moroccan woman on display on her wedding day.

veils, meanwhile, seem to hark back to ancient goddesses whose many draped garments were symbols of femininity and fecundity.

In Morocco, too, dress communicates social values and beliefs even as it indicates wealth and rank. The ceremonial caftan, of oriental origin, provides a contrast between its sober cut (a T-shape) and its magnificent material and embroidered decoration. It is worn for the first time during the wedding, then for family and religious occasions.

Jewish dress in North Africa, meanwhile, could hardly be distinguished from Islamic garments, since the two communities lived on good terms in both town and country. Only ceremonial dress differed, the *kiswat al khibat* being directly inspired by Andalusian models, composed of a large velvet skirt embroidered in concentric rings of gold, topped by a bodice with shirtfront, bolero, and a silk belt. This dress was perhaps the Jewish community's own reminder of the land from which it had been driven six centuries earlier.

With the change in habits, the distinction between the tailored clothing worn in cities and the draped garments worn in rural areas has steadily diminished. Similarly, the originally male *jellaba* was adopted by women in the 1930s for purely practical reasons, somewhat in the way their Western sisters later adopted pants and blue jeans.

Today's top fashion designers, struck by the fullness and opulence of oriental dress, were right to devise modern versions of *chalvar* (harem pants), jellabas, and burnouses. Overturning fashion's slick canons, Azzedine Alaïa unhesitatingly elevated Farida, a model of North African stock, to the rank of top model.

The sari is yet another garment that seems to sum up, all by itself, a civilization with its codes and rites of seduction. Everyone who has ever set foot in India has succumbed to the charm of these long swaths of cloth that women wrap around their bodies with unequaled grace and harmony. Combined with the art of makeup and jewelry, this finery exalts beauty even as it signals the background, caste, and wealth of the wearer. The length of a sari can vary from four to eight yards depending on the region, and can be either tucked tightly around the waist (in Madras) or drawn over the head as a veil (in Muslim-influenced northern India). In Mumbai, women even draw it between their legs to create a type of pant-leg, then pull it over the left shoulder to cover the chest.

The origin of the sari seems to date from the dawn of time. It is perhaps the final incarnation of the graceful drapery adorning the Greco-Buddhist statues of Gandhara. Whatever the case, one thing has never changed: the lack of stitching, which the Hindus perceive as a sign of impurity. In the only concession to fashion, a sari is sometimes worn with a petticoat and a short blouse (*chori*), probably resulting from the combined influence of Islam and the British occupation. This change in habit hardly matters, for the sari remains the perfect symbol of Indian dress, whether of cotton or silk, plain or garished. It is worn by both goddesses and mere mortals. Its fullness and lightness meet the requirements of modesty even as they suggest the charms of a woman's body. Furthermore,

Young woman in a sari. India, Bombay region.

the extraordinary variety of colors and patterns produced by weavers harmoniously counteracts whatever monotony might be produced by the lack of tailoring.

Formerly, the choice of colors scrupulously obeyed a set of rules dictated by region, social station, or ancient caste. Although such customs seem more flexible today, they are far from extinct. Bright colors, particularly appreciated in southern India, remain the privilege of young women; red is suitable for a recent bride; yellow is worn during the rites that follow the birth of a child. Blue and black, on the other hand, are considered unlucky or grim colors, but are sometimes worn to ward off evil. White, the color of religious purity, is above all worn by widows; only Christian women sometimes wear it for a wedding. The production of synthetic colors, of course, has upset the codes of this highly constraining palette. These days, women no longer hesitate to follow their personal inclination, combining luminous colors in an effort to create contrasts of daring boldness. Whether she be a peasant from Rajasthan or a member of high society in New Delhi or Mumbai, an Indian woman is, in a way, her own fashion designer.

Japan, vacillating between highly archaic rigidity and totally frenzied modernity, is perhaps one of the countries that has given dress its great title of nobility. The extreme stylization of jackets, robes, or cloaks, whether outer garment or under garment, endow the human silhouette with a geometric feel found nowhere else. A taste for fabrics themselves, and for their color and pattern, is more important than interest in the body. The pure and almost fleshless profile of Japanese women gives them a deliberately phantom-like appearance. As in India, a relative monotony of cut is based on extreme codification. Even today, young women wear a kimono with very long sleeves, closed by a high sash that covers the chest, whereas married women wear sleeves less full and a sash worn below the breasts. Finally, geishas knot their sashes low and loosely in order to display their shape. The very aesthetics of kimonos can only be grasped via seasonal coding,

Southern Indian woman wearing gold hair ornaments.

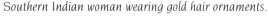

Traditional geishas. Japan, 1875. Hand-colored photograph by Felice Beato.

as conveyed by catalogues: pale green on a dark ground is suited to the month of January, for instance, while pink on a blue ground is appropriate for October. Good taste in Japan means stressing not the shape of the body, but rather the link that binds the individual to surrounding nature—a woman is an ethereal creature as graceful as a flower, as fragile as a reed.

Although poorly adapted to modern lifestyles, kimonos are resurfacing in Western fashion derived from Japan. "Deconstructivism" plays on the fullness of fabrics and can be detected in the spare, supremely elegant designs of the likes of Yohji Yamamoto and the destructured insect dresses by Issey Miyake.

In this land where jewelry strangely disappeared in ancient times, dress finds its natural extension in hair and makeup. A seventeenth-century shogun's decree established the aesthetic ideal of "a very white face in the flickering light of a lantern." Traditional makeup played on a noticeably theatrical three-color scheme (carmine-red lips on a white face with eyebrows drawn in black), but is only used today in the "shady" milieu of red-light districts and show business. Hair, in the form of chignons—thickened with camellia oil, divided into four or five loops coiled on top of the head, down the sides, or on the nape of the neck—epitomizes the absolute sophistication of Japanese refinement. The geisha, that archetype of the woman-child halfway between wife and doll, continues to fire the imagination of fashion designers such as Kenzo from Japan and Jean-Paul Gaultier from France, not forgetting Alexander McQueen from Britain.

"Exotic" garments have now invaded Western wardrobes, from anoraks to ponchos, sarongs, boubous (African dresses), pushtins (fleece-lined leather coats), kimonos, jellabas, burnouses, chalvar (harem pants), and so on. They are like so many accessories that we have adopted, subverted, reinvented. This greedy "appropriation of textiles" is far from new. In the early 1900s, after visiting the Victoria & Albert Museum in London, where he marveled at a collection of Indian turbans, Paul Poiret presented his first oriental collection to corseted Parisian ladies of the day. The shock was enormous. True enough, this was not the first revolution triggered by Poiret the "explorer-designer." Having joined in 1901 the famous Worth fashion house—which dressed the crowned heads of old Europe—Poiret created an immediate scandal by designing a kimono cloak, a vast square of dark wool edged with black satin

Jean-Paul Gaultier's "Mongol" collection, 1994–1995.

bias trimming. The simple cut was countered by rich decoration: the sleeves remained wide to the bottom, ending with embroidery that imitated the sleeves of Chinese cloaks. Poiret had not yet realized that he was establishing the foundations of twentieth-century fashion. Whether changing modern woman into a sultaness or an odalisque straight out of A Thousand and One Nights, he was freeing her from her corset even as he was reinvigorating his own vision with new inspiration. Thanks to Poiret, the era of mélanges had arrived—the Persia of Isfahan met the China of Confucius, recollections of Marrakech merged with the silks of Pondicherry. There was no logic in any of that, but rather a tribute tinged with wonder by a designer faced with different, strange, colorful cultures. An occasional colleague of Poiret's, Mariano Fortuny, displayed the same "geographical and chronological exoticism," to borrow the phrase so rightly used by Sylvie Legrand-Rossi in Touches d'Exotisme (Paris, 1998). Cut from luxurious silks imported from China, India, and Japan, Fortuny's clothes were equally inspired by the Greek chiton, the North African burnous, the Coptic tunic, and the Japanese kimono. Nearly a half-century later, the scene would change: orientalism finally came out of society salons and hit the street and college campuses. Behind this wave was a nonconformist, disillusioned youth movement, thanks to which clothes became ideological—fashion, with its "marketing decisions," was definitely out. It was a time of travel, of a search for new sensory and spiritual experiences. Kabul, Kathmandu, Tangier, and Los Angeles were the new paradises for hippie communities in search of an identity. Eyes were lined with kohl, Indian scarves were drenched in patchouli oil, Mexican ponchos were worn over jeans, Afghan pushtins went with wooden clogs. A veritable ethnic patchwork, this blending of contradictory influences tried to reconcile Mao's China with Gandhi's India, Che's revolution with the West's pop music.

As might be expected, professional fashion designers soon joined the swirl of this "silk and chiffon orientalism." Star models on the pages of glossy magazines henceforth posed against backgrounds of desert or steppes, tropical beach or harem. The French magazine *Elle* went so far as to send top models to rugged Afghanistan—immortalized by Peter Knapp's camera, young women dressed in "nomad-style" caps and jackets posed against the magnificent setting of Bamiyan Valley, protected by its two Buddhas.

Although street fashion continued to prevail, grand fashion designers and stylists proposed their own modern, radical vision of a constantly evolving exoticism. Kenzo, a young Japanese designer who moved to Paris, blithely mingled all folk cultures without rejecting his own—under his aegis, a kimono could flirt with harem pants and a Romanian tunic. Yves Saint-Laurent, who grew up in Morocco, also invented new ethnic combinations. His famous "Bambara" gowns and "African" collection in Spring/Summer 1967 radically changed the haute-couture approach; for the first time, raffia and linen were embroidered with beads of wood and glass, creating a new kind of "poor man's" lavishness. In 1992, meanwhile, Christian Lacroix designed an evening dress wittily called "Kiss Me Dogon": the leather and gilded metal bodice was openly inspired by the jewelry and little bronze sculptures cast in the lost-wax method by several ethnic groups in West Africa. African inspiration could also be felt in Azzedine Alaïa's "Masai" collections and in John Galliano's multiple ethnological allusions to the Dinka tribe of southern Sudan by decorating his evening gowns with corsets of colored beads. Yet even within the same collection (Spring/Summer 1997), Galliano also drew inspiration from China, namely Shanghai of the 1930s, with his fur-trimmed sheath dresses slit high up the side. The nomadic, mestizo world of Dries van Noten, on the other hand, looks to the steppes and mountains of Tibet, to the legendary silk route. Coarse materials are combined with the most refined fabrics. Jean-Paul Gaultier's "Mongol" collection in Fall/Winter 1994–1995 went even further with "Eskimo," which combined ethnic diversity with androgyny—his cloak-peignoirs could be worn by both men and women, sounding the death knell of sexual differentiation in Western clothing. Fashion's enfant terrible will remain forever etched in memories as the hybrid designer par excellence. Gaultier's highly recognizable style insolently and brilliantly shakes up past and present, habits and sexes, materials and supports. He has brought exoticism to the entire body—a body painted, scarred, pierced, and exalted, as magnificently illustrated by the "Tattooing and Piercing" ready-to-wear show presented in Spring/Summer 1994. From street to haute couture and from ritual to fashion, we have decidedly come full circle.

Above:
Bride in Tangier, 1989.
Photograph by Toni Catany, *Novia.*

Right:
Silver buckle. Tunisia. Diam., 7″.
Colette and Jean-Pierre Ghysels's collection.

Left:
Moroccan woman wearing an amber necklace.

Above:
Tiznit (Berber) woman's necklace. Morocco. Silver, amber, and shells.
Length, 17". Colette and Jean-Pierre Ghysels's collection.

Following pages:
(left) Sudanese woman.
(right) Peul woman from Niger.

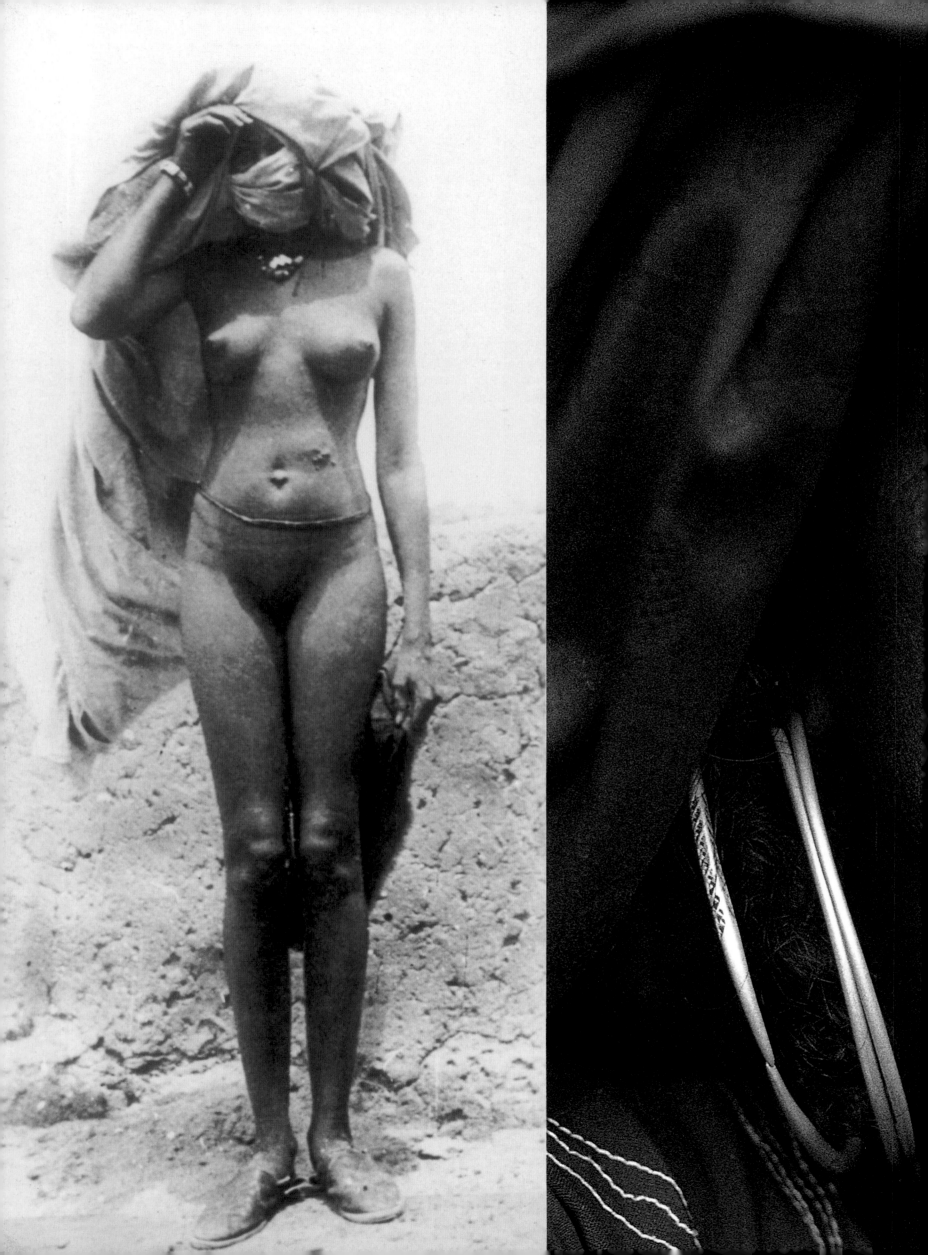

Above:
Short evening dress by Yves Saint Laurent.
Spring/Summer 1967 haute-couture collection.

Right:
Seduction dance in Chad.

Following pages:
Young Masai warrior.

Above:
Karamayong men's helmet. Clay, hair, and ostrich feathers.
Kenya. Height, 11³/⁴". Colette and Jean-Pierre Ghysels's collection.

Right:
Young Mangbetu woman wearing the characteristic headdress
of this ethnic group. Zaire.

Following pages:
Face painting for the sacred oxen festival.
Angola, Huila region.

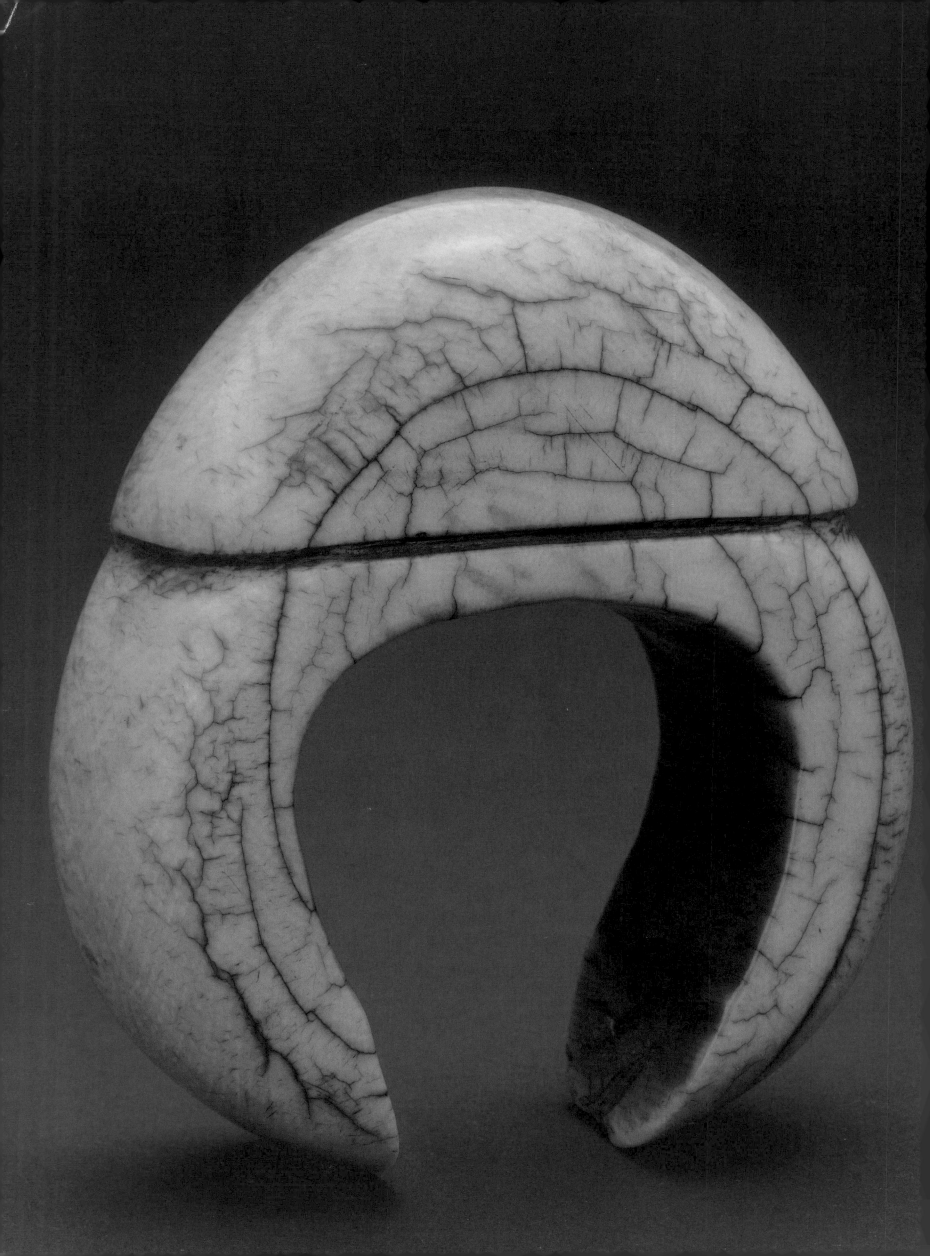

Preceding pages:
(left) Ivory Bamum bracelet. Cameroon.
Height, 4¹ᐟ⁴″. Colette and Jean-Pierre Ghysels's collection.
(right) Lahobé woman. Senegal, circa 1900.

Above:
Nancy Cunnard with her African bracelets,
photographed in 1926 by Man Ray.

Right:
Djokélébalé anklet from the Kota of Gabon.
Brass. Diam., 4¹ᐟ⁴″. Barbier-Mueller Museum, Geneva.

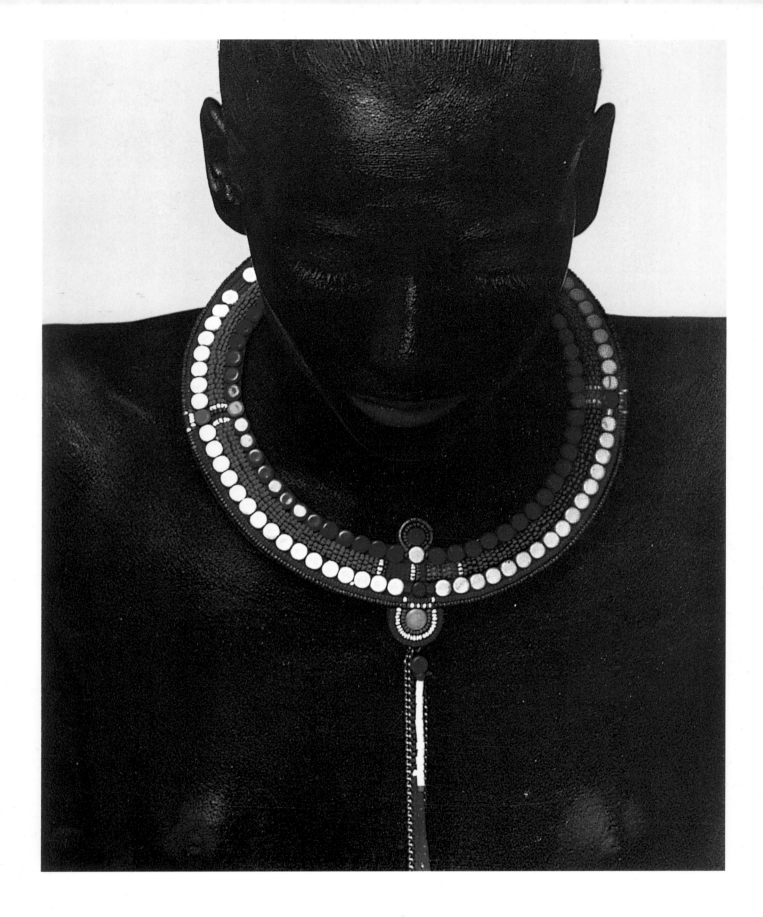

Above:
Woman painted by Serge Lutens
wearing a Zulu necklace, 1967.

Right:
Young woman with multiple pearl necklaces.
Angola, Huila region.

Left:
Surma man
prepared for the
Donga battles.
Ethiopia.

Right:
Masai warrior.

Following pages:
(left) Bronze women's
anklet. Height, 8¼".
Burkina Fasso,
Gourounsi.
Colette and Jean-Pierre
Ghysels's collection.
(right) Ekeledi dancers.

Above:
Naomi Campbell by Paolo Roversi. Interpretation of a traditional coiffure
with spiked braids, in fashion in Burkina Fasso.

Right:
Onile Gogoro or akaba. Free-standing or ladder coiffure.
Style adopted by women of high standing for major social occasions.

Following pages:
(left) Masai woman with a large beaded necklace, an insignia of her rank.
(right) Gold Peul earrings. Mali.
Height, 3¹/²". Colette and Jean-Pierre Ghysels's collection.

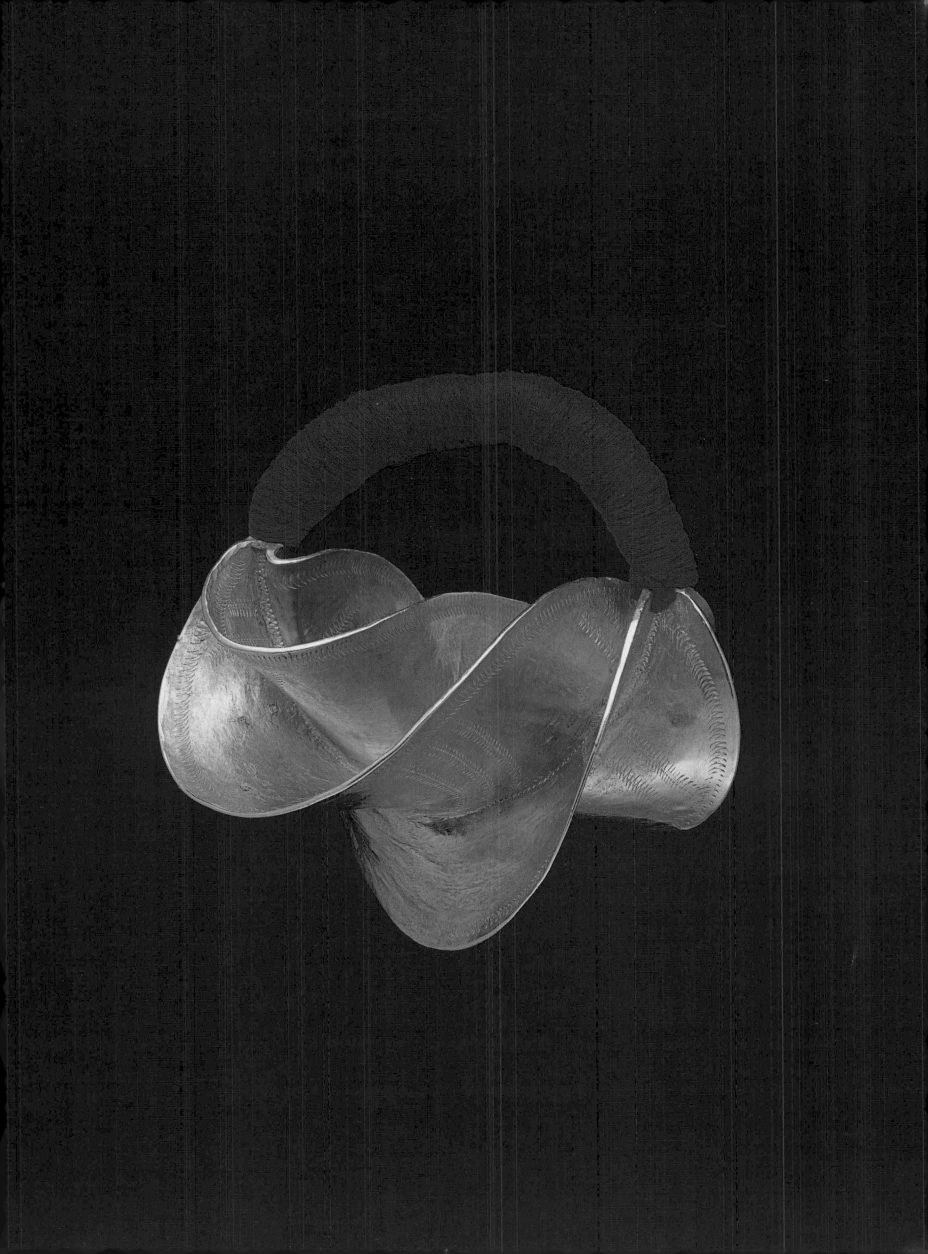

Left:
Xuly-Bêt's 1999
Spring/Summer collection.

Right:
Nubian woman. Egypt, 1880.

Following pages:
(left) Pendant from a Bedouin
headdress, made of gold,
turquoise, beads, and textile.
Saudi Arabia, Najd.
Height, 6¹/⁴".
Colette and Jean-Pierre
Ghysels's collection.
(right) Bedouin woman from
the Al-Yami tribe in the
Najran region (Yemen-Saudi
Arabian border).

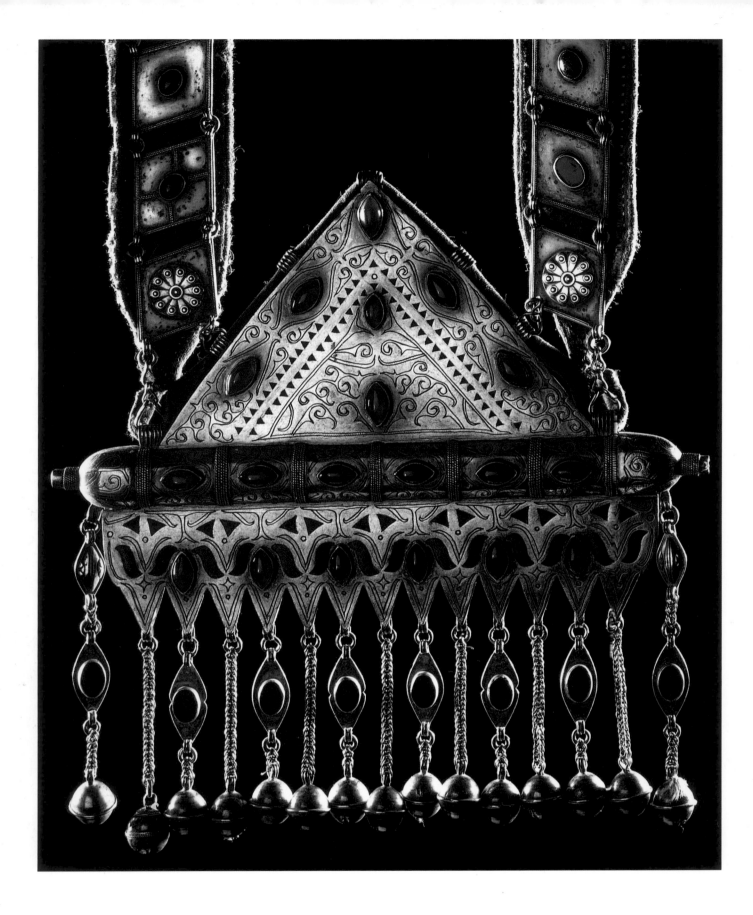

Above:
A Tekke tumar or amulet-holder; verses for the Koran are placed in the central tube, which opens up. Solid silver with gilded designs, cornelian, green and red baize, thick fabric strap. Turkmenia. Length, 28". Barbier-Mueller Museum, Geneva.

Right:
Uzbek woman wearing a traditional *ikat* dress.

Following pages:
(left) Young Indian woman from Rajasthan, with jewels on her feet and a headdress decorated with small mirrors.
(right) Torque worn by the Bhils, in the Kush (India, Gujarat region).
Wound silver wire. Width, 7³ᐟ⁴". Barbier-Mueller Museum, Geneva.

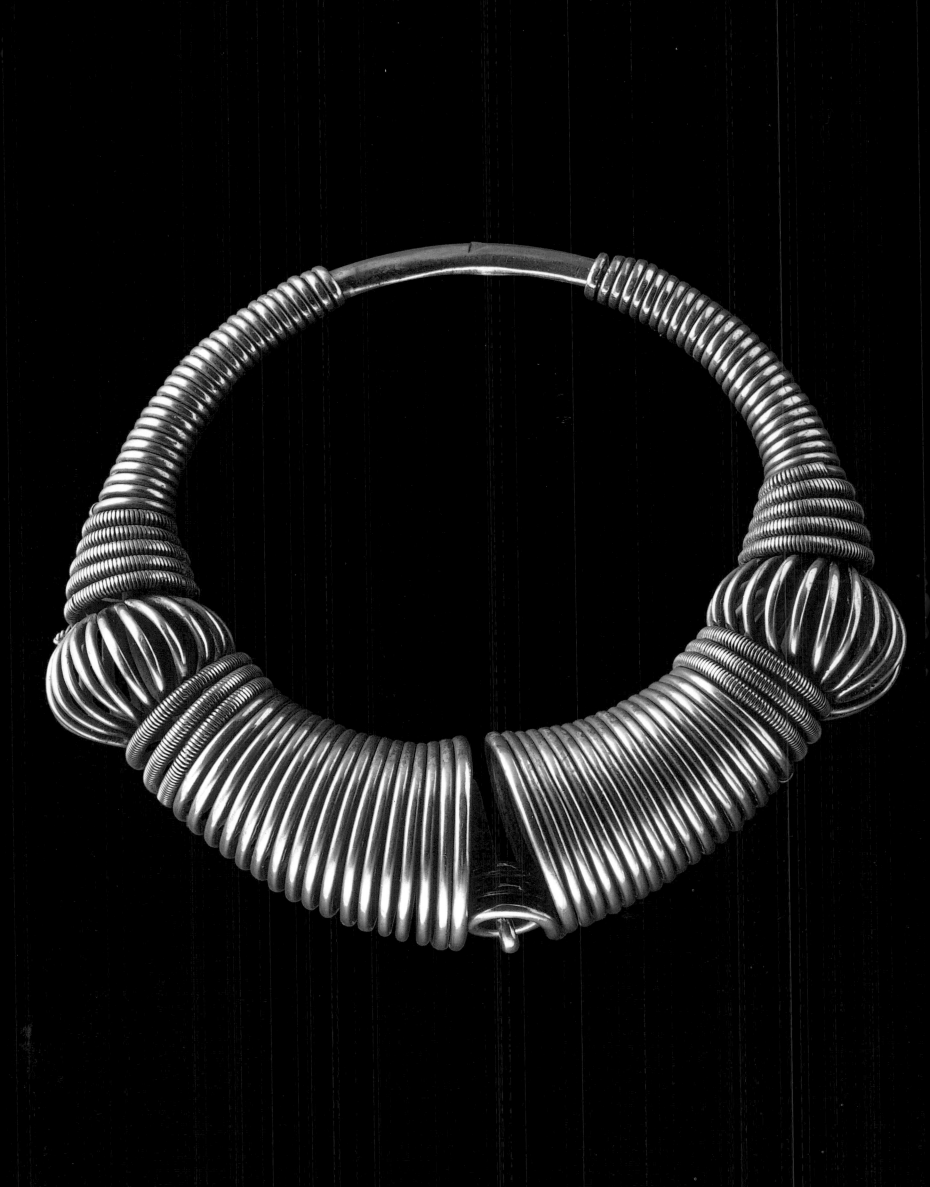

Above:
Tattooed hand. Rabal tribe, Gujurat desert.

Right:
Young Indian woman adorned for a ceremony. India, Bombay, 1993.

Following pages:
(left) Anklets worn by Shekhavati women. Hammered silver.
India, northwestern Rajasthan. Width, 5¹ᐟ²″. Barbier-Mueller Museum, Geneva.
(right) Jewels worn by women during the Gangaur festival at Kishangahr, Rajasthan.

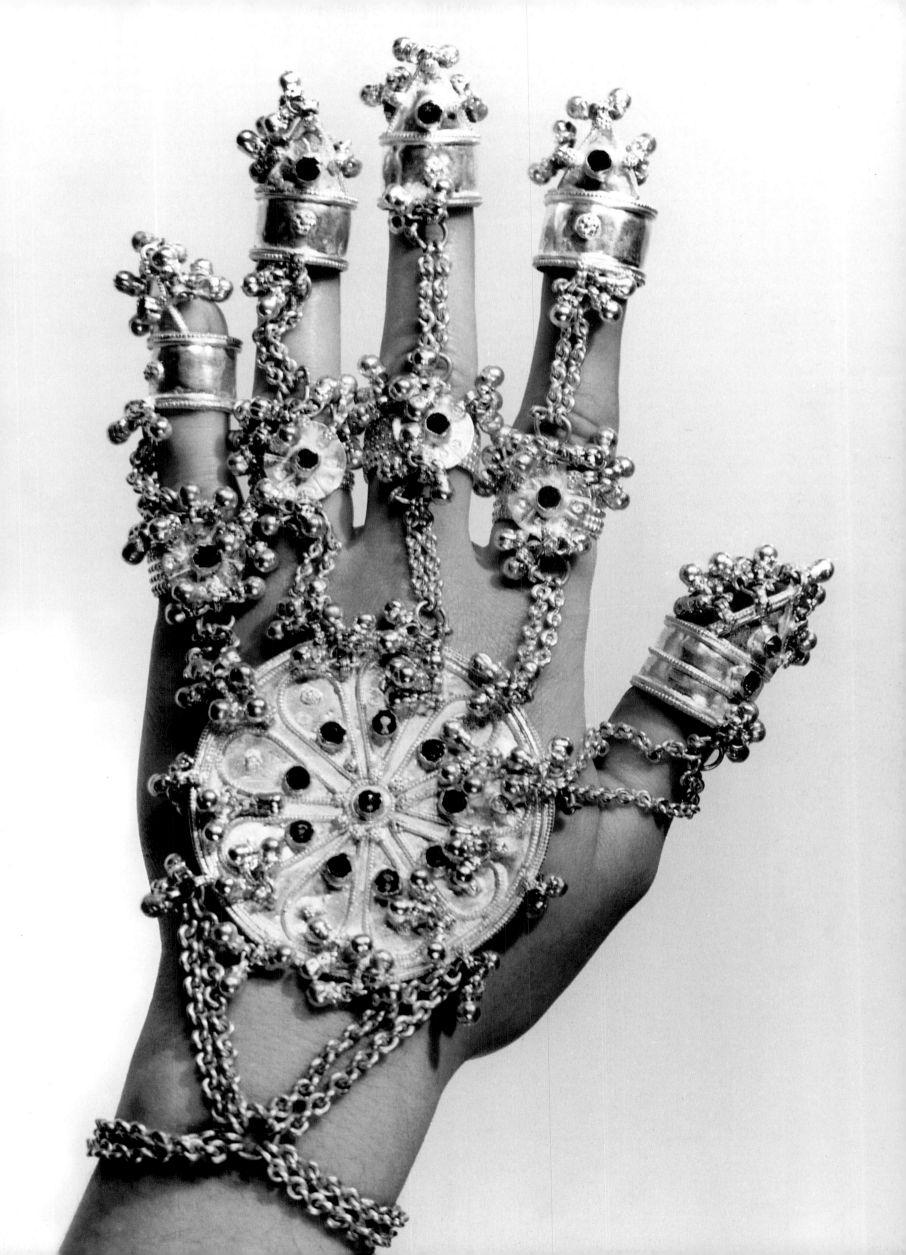

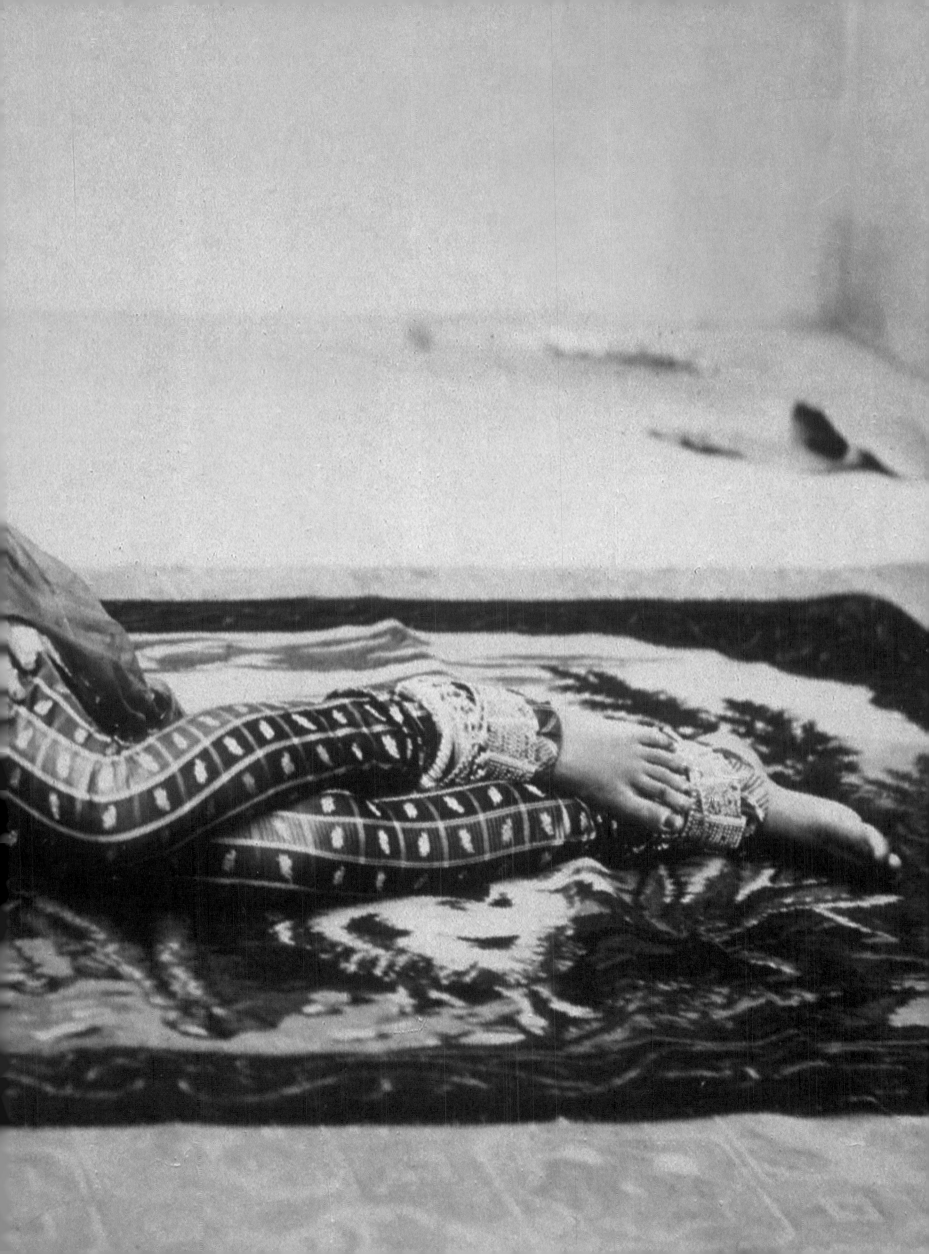

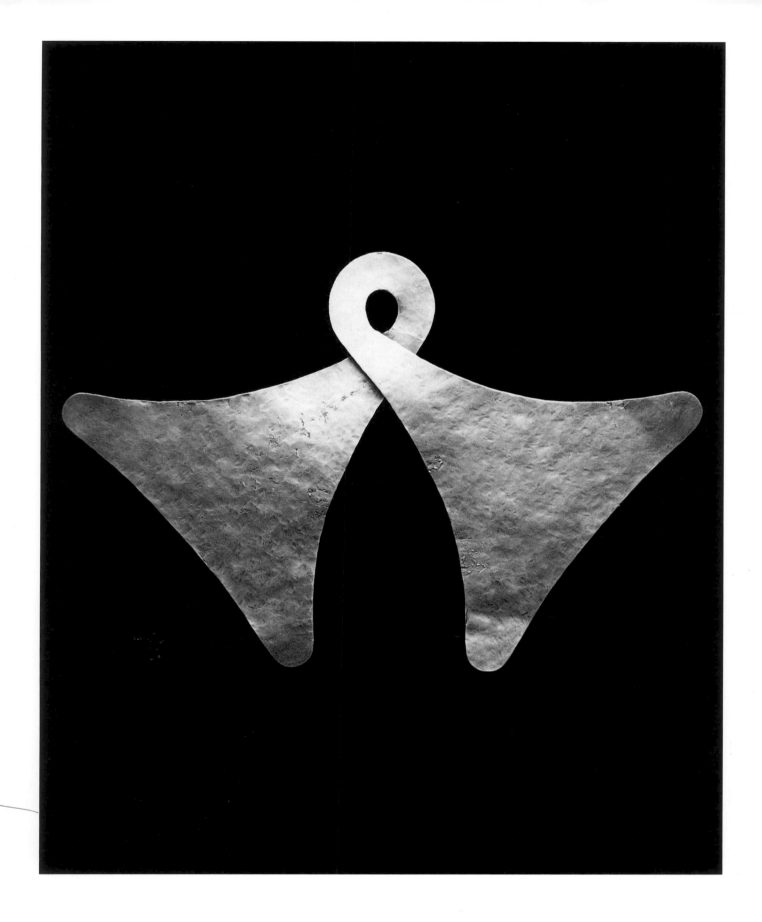

Pages 90–91:
(left) Indian women.
(right) Silver hand ornament with pieces of colored glass.

Preceding pages:
A 19th-century Indian "odalisque."

Above:
Maranga pendant made from a thick sheet of hammered, almost pure gold.
Indonesia, Sonde region, Sumba Island. Length, 12". Barbier-Mueller Museum, Geneva.

Right:
Hoa Meo woman. North Vietnam.

Left:
Issey Miyake, 1997.
Kimono jacket with flared sleeves,
made of quilted velvet with top-
stitch ng, lined with yellow silk;
matching skirt slit up the sides.

Right
Phine Tao-Yao woman. North
Vietnam, Tonkin.

*Follo*ing pages:*
(left) Khmer dance.
Cambodia, 1996.
(right) Hindu worshiper, his face
covered with prayers.

Preceding pages:
(left) "Giraffe-woman" tin torque. Burma, Padaung.
Height, 6". Colette and Jean-Pierre Ghysels's collection.
(right) Young Man Tien woman. North Vietnam, Upper Tonkin, 1920.

Left:
Chinese woman from the region of Yunnan.

Above:
Naga necklace made of brass, cornelian beads, shells, and glass.
Northern India. Length, 29¹/₂". Barbier-Muller Museum, Geneva.

Above:
Kimono created by Fortuny. Moiré *wabi*-colored Japanese silk satin, hand-painted with a prunus design, an Oriental *memento mori,* in which the trees offers its buds, flowers, and fruits before dying.

Right:
A geisha, representing the quintessence of Japanese refinement. Japan, 1956.

Above:
Jean-Paul Gaultier's 1999 ready-to-wear fashion show.

Right:
Geisha revealing her bared neck, the ultimate in erotic seduction.

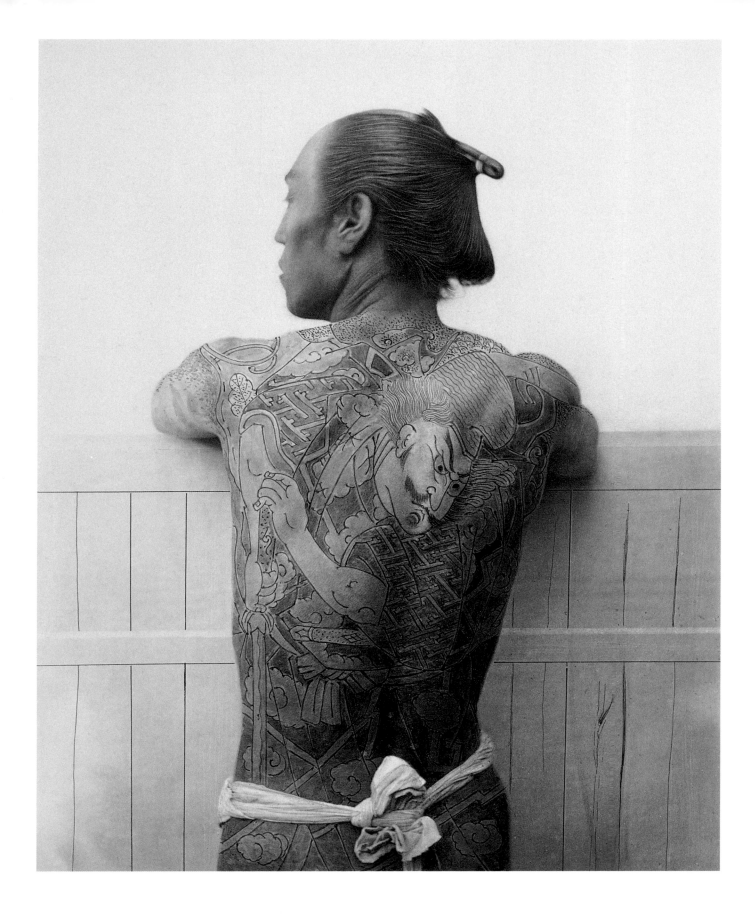

Above:
An entirely tattooed groom. Circa 1867.

Right:
Bride's silk kimono with a pattern obtained from various techniques
(weaving, embroidery, tie-dying), lined with red silk.

Following pages:
Funeral of Changjiao Miao in China.

Preceding pages:
(left) Gold and turquoise headdress pendant. Tibet, Lhasa.
Height, 6". Colette and Jean-Pierre Ghysels's collection.
(right) Bedecked Yi women, China.

Above:
Maori pendant (*hei tiki*). Jadeite (or "greenstone").
Polynesia, New Zealand. Height, 4". Barbier-Mueller Museum, Geneva.

Right:
Old Maori with facial tattoos. Polynesia, New Zealand.

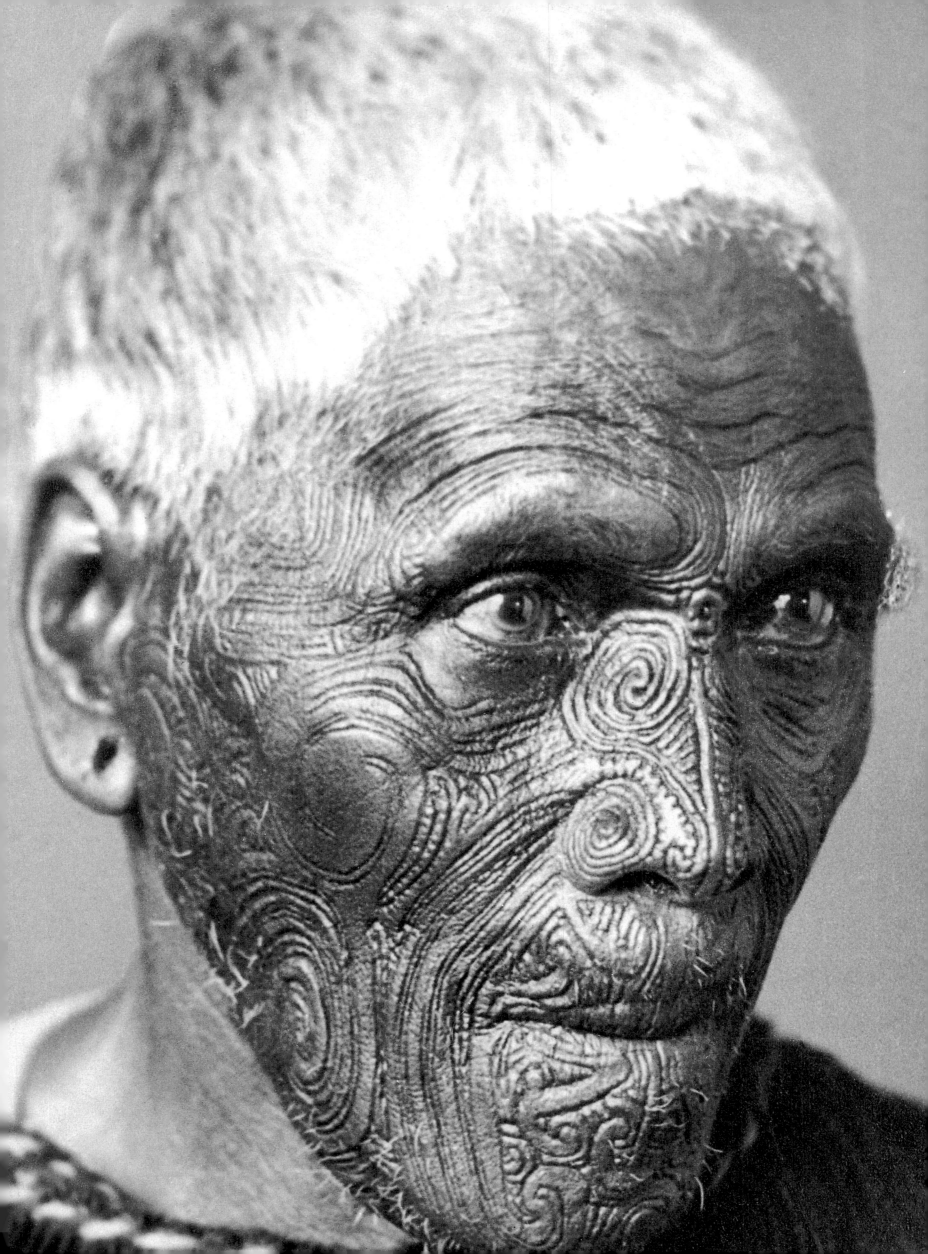

Above:
Tattooed Tahitian man.
Photograph by Gian Paolo Barbieri.

Right:
Hawaiian necklace (*leiniho palaoa*). Braided human hair, sailor's ivory pendant.
Polynesia. Height, 14". Barbier-Mueller Museum, Geneva.

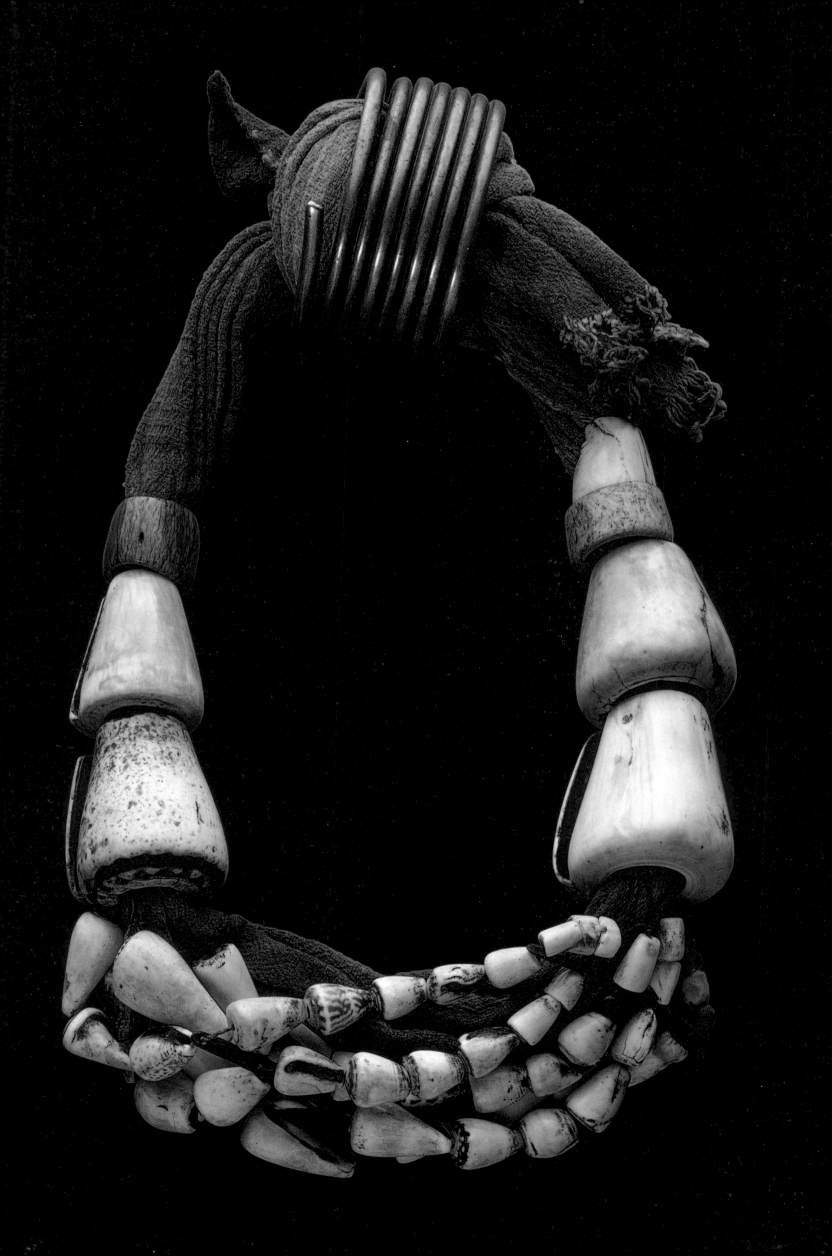

Left:
Woman's belt (*sangilot*), made of shells, fabric, and brass wire by the
Bontoc from the north of Luçon Island. Philippines. Diam., 13″.
Barbier-Mueller Museum, Geneva.

Above:
New Guinean woman. 1897.

Above:
Christian Dior's 1997 haute-couture collection, photographed by Paolo Roversi.

Right:
Face painted with the sign of the Bos. Brazil, Rio Nhamunda.

Following pages:
(left) Indian woman wearing a traditional outfit of the Mapuche community.
(right) *Tupu,* silver piece. Buckle traditionally worn by Mapuche women. 13″, 3.3 oz.

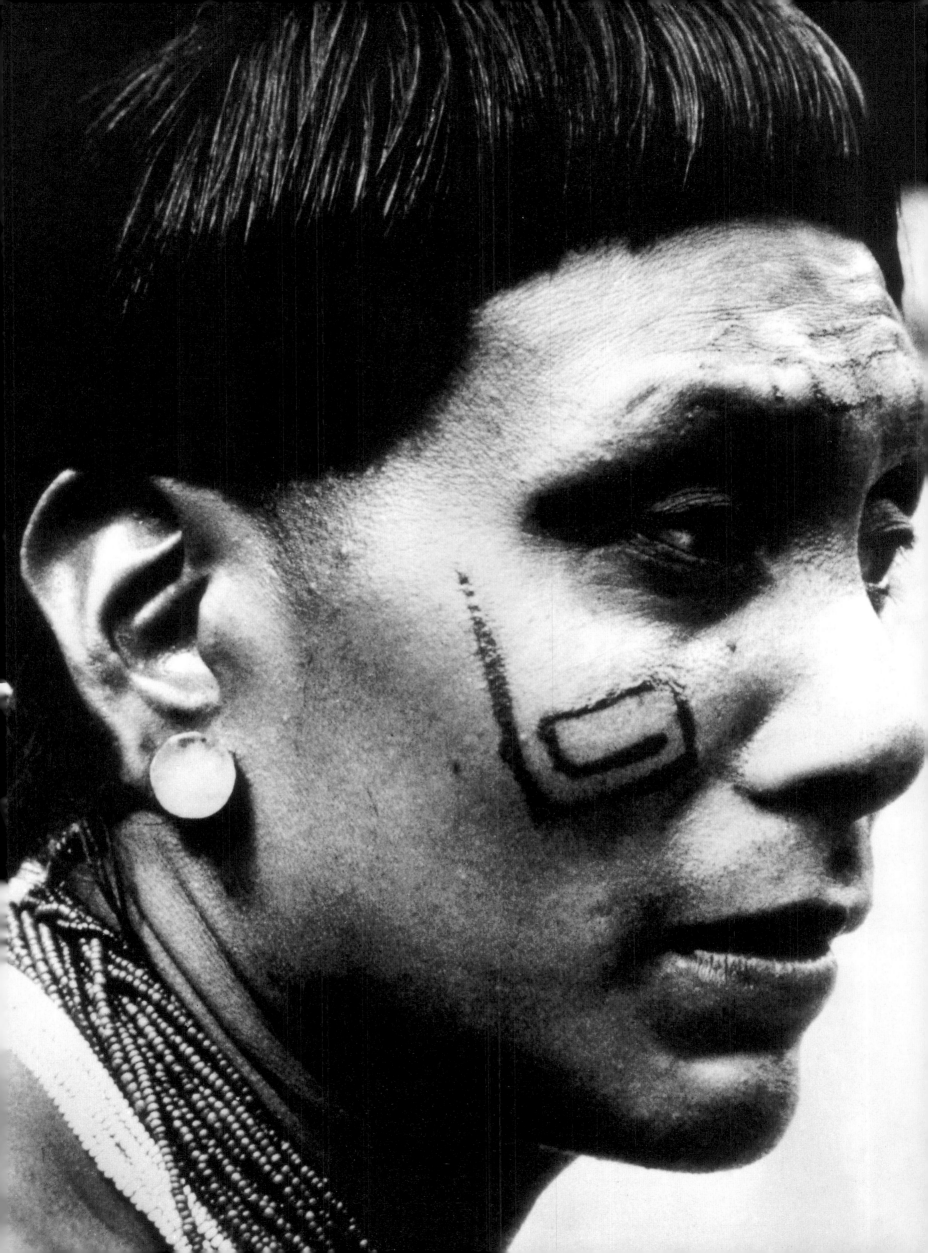

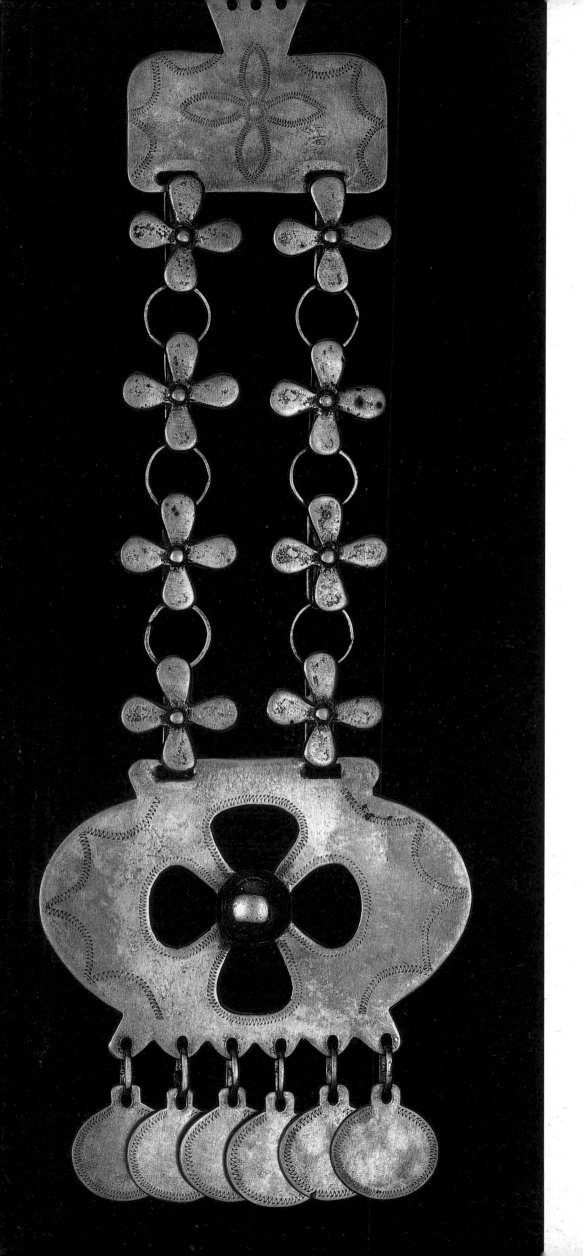

Left:
Combapatan peasant. Peru, Cuzco region, 1934.

Above:
Frida Kahlo in a traditional Mexican outfit.

Following pages:
Street scene in Guatemala, by Deborah Turbeville.

Left:
Feathered labret. Brazil, Maranhao region, Urubu-Ka'apor.

Above:
Dandy from the Piegan region. Photograph by Edward Curtis, 1900.

Above:
Man's leather shirt. Great Plains Indians (Blackfoot).

Right:
Sioux woman wearing a necklace of bone beads and ear pendants made of shells and bone. Photograph by Edward Curtis, circa 1900.

ELEMENTS OF BIBLIOGRAPHY

On the body:

Borel, F., *Le vêtement incarné, Les métamorphoses du corps* (Paris: Calmann-Lévy, 1992).

Falgayrettes-Leveau, C., *Corps sublimes* (Paris: Musée Dapper, 1994).

Heuze, S. (ed.), *Changer le corps?* (Paris: La Musardine, 2000).

On skin:

Borel, F., *Le vêtement incarné, Les métamorphoses du corps* (Paris: Calmann-Lévy, 1992).

Caruchet, W., *Tatouages et tatoués* (Paris: Tchou, 1976).

Certeau, M., "Des outils pour écrire le corps," *Traverses*, April 1979.

Ebin, V., *Corps décorés* (Paris: Chêne, 1979).

Faris, J.-C., *Nuba Personal Art* (Toronto: University of Toronto Press, 1972).

Fischer, A., *Fastueuse Afrique* (Paris: Chêne, 1984).

Lévi-Strauss, C., *Tristes Tropiques* (Paris: Plon, 1955).

Maertens, J.T., "Le dessein sur la peau," *Ritologiques* 1 (Paris: Aubier, 1978).

Pons, P., *Peau de brocart: Le corps tatoué au Japon* (Paris: Seuil, 2000).

Thévoz, M., *Le Corps peint* (Geneva: Skira, 1984).

Thomas, N., *Oceanic Art* (London: Thames & Hudson, 1995).

On jewelry:

Barbier, J.-P., *Art du Nagaland* (Geneva: Barbier-Mueller Museum, 1982).

Barbier, J.-P., and M. Butor, *Parure* (Paris: Imprimerie Nationale, 1994).

Besancenot, J., *Bijoux arabes et berbères du Maroc* (Casablanca: Éditions de la Cigogne, 1953).

Borel, F., *Orfèvres lointains, Bijoux d'Afrique, d'Asie, d'Océanie et d'Amérique* (Paris: Hazan, 1995).

Camps-Fabrer, H., *Bijoux berbères d'Algérie* (Aix-en-Provence: Édisud, 1990).

Cerval, Marguerite de, et al., *Dictionnaire international du bijou* (Paris: Éditions du Regard, 1998).

Fischer, A., *Fastueuse Afrique* (Paris: Chêne, 1984).

Garrard, T.F., *Or d'Afrique, Bijoux et Parures du Ghana, Côte d'Ivoire, Mali et Sénégal de la collection du Musée Barbier-Mueller* (Paris: Hazan, 1990).

Rodgers, S., *L'Or des îles, Bijoux et Ornements d'Indonésie, de Malaisie, et des Philippines dans les collections du Musée Barbier-Mueller de Genève* (Geneva: Éditions du Musée Barbier-Mueller, 1991).

On dress:

Art pictural des Pygmées (Geneva: Barbier-Mueller Museum, 1990).

Baudot, F., *Mode du Siècle* (Paris: Éditions Assouline, 1999).

Coquet, M., *Textiles africains* (Paris: Société Nouvelle Adam Biro, 1993).

Ducor, J., and J. Watts, *Saris de l'Inde* (Geneva: Éditions Olizane, 1996).

Geoffroy-Schneiter, B., *Geishas* (Paris: Éditions Assouline, 2000).

Noces tissées, noces brodées, parures et costumes féminins de Tunisie (Paris: Éditions Joël Cuénot 1995).

Splendeurs du Maro (Tervuren: Musée royal de l'Afrique centrale, 1998).

Touches d'exotisme, XIVᵉ-XXᵉ siècles (Paris: Union Centrale des Arts Décoratifs, Musée de la mode et du textile, 1998).

PHOTOGRAPHIC CREDITS

ACKNOWLEDGMENTS
My warm thanks go to the entire team at Les Éditions Assouline who helped to bring this project to fruition, notably Véronique Billiotte for her valuable picture research, Mathilde Dupuy d'Angeac for her inspired book design, and Julie David for her unflagging, efficient support. Meanwhile, Laurent and Cassandre Schneiter were intimate partners, as usual, in this "new adventure."
The publisher wishes to thank the Barbier-Mueller Museum in Geneva, Colette and Jean-Pierre Ghysels, Guy Joubert and André Magnin for their kind collaboration.